Helping Children with Dyspraxia

Helping Children with Dyspraxia

Maureen Boon

Jessica Kingsley Publishers
London and Philadelphia

First published in the United Kingdom in 2001 by
Jessica Kingsley Publishers Ltd,
116 Pentonville Road,
London N1 9JB,
England
and
325 Chestnut Street,
Philadelphia, PA 19106, USA.

www.jkp.com

Second impression 2002

Library of Congress Cataloging in Publication Data
A CIP catalog record for this book is available from the Library of Congress

British Library Cataloguing in Publication Data
A CIP catalogue record for this book is available from the British Library

ISBN 1 85302 881 9

Printed and Bound in Great Britain by
Athenaeum Press, Gateshead, Tyne and Wear

Contents

Acknowledgements

I would like to thank the staff at Vranch House who were so helpful to me in writing this book. In particular I would like to thank Penny Hale, superintendent physiotherapist, and her staff for allowing me to watch and participate in their groups. Thanks also to Penny Hale and Lynn Dyson, speech and language therapist, for reading the manuscript and making helpful and constructive comments. I am grateful, too, to Dr Geoff Meek, lecturer in exercise and sport sciences at St Luke's Campus at the University of Exeter, and his students for allowing me to share in their work with the children.

In particular I must thank the parents who shared their experiences with me and allowed me to take photographs. Most of all, thanks are due to the children who attend Vranch House Centre and work so hard with good humour and enthusiasm.

CHAPTER I

What is Dyspraxia?

If you ask different professionals what dyspraxia is, you get different answers, depending on their field of expertise. A physiotherapist would probably say that the child in question has impaired motor performance that is not linked to any known clinical cause. A speech and language therapist might say that the child has a motor difficulty that affects that initiating and sequencing of sounds and words. A teacher might well describe the dyspraxic child as inattentive and lacking in concentration skills. A parent might describe his or her child as clumsy and disorganised and having poor co-ordination. All might be descriptions of the same child.

The Dyspraxia Foundation (1998) defines dyspraxia as 'an impairment or immaturity of the organisation of movement. Associated with this there may be problems of language, perception and thought.'

The term 'dyspraxia' has been recognised for some time. The word is derived from the Greek and means literally the poor performance of movements. It was defined in *The American Illustrated Medical Dictionary* in 1947 as 'partial loss of ability to perform co-ordinated movements' (Dorland 1947, p.465). In the same year *The New Dictionary of Psychology* gave the definition, 'impairment of well-established habits as a consequence of a stroke or of other pathologies of the central nervous system' (Harriman 1947, p.113). It is clear that at that time the meaning of 'dyspraxia' was somewhat different from our understanding today. Nowadays the term often used is the more specific 'developmental dyspraxia', implying that the condition is due to the immature development of motor abilities.

Portwood defines dyspraxia as 'motor difficulties caused by perceptual problems, especially visual-motor and kinaesthetic-motor difficulties' (Portwood 1996, p.15). McKinlay says, 'Dyspraxia is a *delay* or *disorder* of the planning and/or execution of complex movements. It may be developmental – part of a child's make-up – or it can be acquired at any stage in life as the result of brain illness or injury' (McKinlay 1998, p.9). I asked my colleagues working with dyspraxic children for their definitions.

A PHYSIOTHERAPIST'S DEFINITION

Children with dyspraxia should demonstrate no hard neuro-logical signs (i.e. damage of the central nervous system). Their motor performance should be at a level lower than that expected of their general learning abilities; i.e. their motor performance is out of step with their intellectual functioning.

ANOTHER PHYSIOTHERAPIST'S DEFINITION

This physiotherapist makes a distinction between developmental co-ordination disorder and dyspraxia:

Developmental co-ordination disorder is an umbrella term for a range of movement disorders that is not due to any obvious neurological or orthopaedic condition. There may be associated difficulties with social skills, attention control, self-help skills and perceptual skills.

Dyspraxia is a specific movement disorder characterised by difficulty in performing an unlearned complex motor skill that may be due to difficulty with ideation, or motor planning and sequencing or the execution of the task. The disorder is often associated with poor visual or auditory and/or kinaesthetic perception.

Other disorders that she includes under developmental co-ordin-ation disorder are general global delay (i.e. learning difficulties), poor muscle tone, attention deficit/hyperactivity disorder (ADHD) and general poor attention control.

AN OCCUPATIONAL THERAPIST'S DEFINITION

Children with dyspraxia have motor co-ordination problems. They often present as having problems with the organisation and execution of gross and fine movement. They often have associated difficulties with perceptual and organisational skills and may have receptive and expressive language problems.

A SPEECH AND LANGUAGE THERAPIST'S DEFINITION

'Dyspraxia' is a term used to describe a motor problem that causes difficulty with initiation and/or sequencing of the muscle movements required to produce voice and/or speech. It is essentially a problem of not being able voluntarily to carry out movements that can easily be carried out involuntarily. A child may not be able to control and sequence breathing and voice and so only produce random vocalisations. He may not be able to move his tongue and lips into the correct positions or sequence of positions to make sounds, words or sentences, even though there is no muscle weakness to prevent this. A child can be observed to be licking his lips without realising whilst playing, but put on the spot and asked to lick his lips he cannot do so. Children who have the range of difficulties associated with dyspraxia often experience social-communication problems and difficulty in understanding the more abstract and subtle parts of language.

A TEACHER'S DEFINITION

Dyspraxia is a movement disorder not caused by a known clinical condition. The children affected are within the normal range of intellectual functioning and have poor hand–eye co-ordination and poor gross motor co-ordination. It can also affect speech.

Terms used to describe dyspraxia

Over the last few years a number of different terms have been used to describe the condition which we would now term 'developmental dyspraxia', as well as other, very similar, conditions:

- clumsy child syndrome
- developmental agnosia and apraxia
- developmental co-ordination disorder (DCD)
- learning difficulties/disabilities/disorders
- minimal cerebral palsy
- minimal cerebral dysfunction
- minimal brain dysfunction
- minimal motor dysfunction
- motor learning difficulties
- neurodevelopmental dysfunction
- perceptual/perceptuo-motor dysfunction
- physical awkwardness
- specific learning difficulties
- sensori-motor dysfunction.

The number of terms used to describe dyspraxia is large and wide-ranging, and some are now used to describe quite different areas of difficulty. 'Specific learning difficulties' is a term now usually taken to mean 'dyslexia' or 'dyscalculia'. Dyslexia describes specific problems with reading and recognising written text, and dyscalculia describes difficulties with numeracy. Some terms are too vague, such as 'learning difficulties', and some are not accurate, such as 'minimal cerebral palsy'. Some are very descriptive but are not in common usage. The term 'developmental co-ordination disorder' is the one most often used, and was described by the American Psychiatric Association in 1987 as a developmental disorder of motor skills (American Psychiatric Association 1987). This was endorsed by the World Health Organisation in 1989. The term is now being used interchangeably with 'developmental dyspraxia', although some use it more widely to include dyspraxia and other movement disorders.

The different types or aspects of dyspraxia

A number of types or aspects of dyspraxia have also been described.

Verbal dyspraxia

With verbal dyspraxia the child has difficulty in actually carrying out the movements needed to produce clear speech. Not *all* children with dyspraxia have difficulties with speech and language. Sometimes the child may have difficulty in actually producing the sounds or may be able to produce them at some times but not at others. He may find copying speech more difficult than when he uses speech spontaneously. Sometimes the child has difficulty in producing the right word at the right time and putting the words in the right order.

Sensory integrative dysfunction

Sensory Integrative Therapy was pioneered by Dr A. Jean Ayres, an American occupational therapist (Ayres 1972). The child with sensory integrative dysfunction has difficulties in sensory integration, which means that she finds it difficult to organise the information received from the sensory apparatus about the interaction of her body with the environment.

That is to say, the difficulty is in making sense of the information received from the senses of hearing, sight, smell, touch and taste and through the proprioception system and the vestibular apparatus. Proprioceptors are nerve endings, or receptors, through which we are aware of our muscles and joints and whether they are bending or stretching. The vestibular apparatus, which is in the inner ear, gives information about movement and our position in space. It is the system through which we are aware of the position of our head in relation to gravity. Through kinaesthetic sensations we become aware of the relationship between body parts, joint positions and movements.

Poor sensory integration may mean that some dyspraxic children are oversensitive to noise or to different textures. Some may not be able to perform certain movements unless they can observe the body part moving. For example, if a child is asked to stretch out an arm in front of him and then asked to place a finger on his nose, he may be able to do this with his eyes open when he can observe the moving hand, but not if he closes his eyes.

Ideational dyspraxia and ideomotor dyspraxia

Ripley, Daines and Barrett describe two areas of difficulty as ideational and ideomotor dyspraxia. With ideational dyspraxia, the child has difficulties in planning sequential co-ordinated movements (Ripley *et al.* 1997, p.5). With ideomotor dyspraxia, the child knows what to do but has difficulties in carrying out a plan of action.

The incidence of dyspraxia

The first time I heard the word 'clumsy' used to describe a group of children was when I was working as a supply teacher in a school for children with physical disabilities in 1978. I was taking lessons for the deputy head, who was on a week's course on 'Teaching the Clumsies'. In 1983 I returned to work at the same school as head of lower school, and at that time this group of children with less severe physical difficulties had become smaller through integration into mainstream schools, and they were rarely referred to as 'clumsy'.

Since 1983 I have worked with children with motor disorders in both special and mainstream schools, and it was only when I moved to my current school, Vranch House, in Devon in 1992 that I heard the term 'dyspraxia' being used commonly and on an everyday basis. In the last ten years 'dyspraxia' has been used more frequently in books and journals and has replaced the awkward, somewhat negative but descriptive word, 'clumsy'.

In 1988–1989 I carried out a study on the integration of children with special needs in mainstream schools in Lancashire (Boon 1993) which involved studying registers of all integrated statemented children in the county and classifying them by special educational need. No mention was made of dyspraxia. One child was described as 'disorganised'. All the others fell under the headings of specific, moderate or severe learning difficulties; sensory, language or physical difficulties; or emotional/behavioural difficulties. Nowadays I would expect a similar study to describe a fair number of children as 'dyspraxic'. At Vranch House the paediatric physiotherapy service sees on average a hundred children from mainstream schools who attend once a week and who live within a reasonable travelling distance of Exeter. Of these currently 38 per cent would be correctly described as dyspraxic; if children with learning difficulties who have dyspraxic features were also included, this would rise to 47 per cent.

In her Durham study Portwood (1996) suggests an incidence of 6 per cent out of the whole population. In their Leeds study Roussounis, Gaussen and Stratton (1987) found that the incidence of 'clumsy children' was 8.5 per cent from a cohort of two hundred children at primary school entry age. In a study of schoolchildren in East Kent, Dussart (1994) found the incidence to be between 3.7 and 6.5 per cent, depending on whether the results were based on the TOMI, or Test of Motor Impairment (Stott, Moyes and Henderson 1984) or on a checklist developed by Dussart for the study. Different estimates are, however, likely to be dependent on the screening measures used. The more recent version of the TOMI is the Movement Assessment Battery for Children, or Movement ABC (Henderson and Sugden 1992). It is commonly used in this country and children who score on or below the 5th percentile are normally considered to be those needing intervention. As the test is standardised, this necessarily means that the incidence will be around 5 per cent.

The ratio of boys to girls has always shown a higher percentage of boys than girls. Gordon and McKinlay (1980) found that of 'clumsy' children referred to the neurology clinics of the children's hospitals in Manchester the ratio of boys to girls was 4 to 1. Portwood (1996) found the ratio to be the same.

Difficulties experienced by children with dyspraxia

Dyspraxic children may experience difficulties in some or all of the following areas.

Gross motor skills

They may move awkwardly and have poor balance and co-ord-ination. They may have difficulties in PE generally. They are likely to have poor ball skills, when using either hands or feet for skills such as catching and throwing and kicking a ball.

Fine motor skills

They may find holding pencils and pens difficult, and their writing and drawing may be poorly formed. They may find cutlery and other mealtime utensils hard to manage and make a mess. Dressing skills such as fastening zips, buttons and laces may be very difficult or impossible. They may find it difficult to thread beads, build with small bricks or use other toys that need reasonably fine motor skills.

Speech and language

They may have unclear speech, which may be immature. They may find it difficult to put their ideas into words. They sometimes seem to miss or not understand what is said to them.

Social skills

They may find it difficult to make friends and to be part of a group. Their difficulty with motor skills will mean that they are not often chosen to play games where these skills are necessary.

Attention and concentration

They find it difficult to concentrate for very long. They may be easily distracted by noises, things happening outside the classroom window or other activities going on around them. They may find it difficult to sit still.

Learning

They may have difficulties with reading, spelling and maths, which may be linked to poor visual-perceptual skills.

Visual motor skills

They may find it difficult to copy pictures, patterns, writing or movements. They may have poor spatial awareness.

CHAPTER 2

What Causes Dyspraxia?

It is not clearly known what causes dyspraxia. It appears to be a developmental delay specifically in areas affecting motor function, which may involve gross motor, fine motor or articulatory skills. Some dyspraxic children also have other learning difficulties, whilst some are of average or above-average intelligence. Some practitioners would argue that a child who has a moderate general learning difficulty is effectively delayed globally and therefore is not dyspraxic. However, treatment has also proved effective with these children.

At Vranch House about a quarter of the dyspraxic children have other learning difficulties, but it is nevertheless their motor difficulties that have caused them to be referred following problems at school in these areas. Wedell points out that 'the development of sensory and motor organisation starts before language development' (Wedell 1973, p.46). It is clear that any delays in sensory and motor organisation will affect all areas of subsequent learning. In some instances it is difficult to say how much a child's motor disorder has contributed to her other learning difficulties.

Reasons given for Dyspraxia

The Dyspraxia Foundation (1998) says that 'For most children there is no known cause, although it is thought to be an immaturity of neurone development in the brain rather than brain damage. Dyspraxic children have no clinical neurological abnormality to explain their condition.' Madeleine Portwood agrees with this: 'Dyspraxia results when parts of the brain have failed to mature properly...[it] is the result of neurological immaturity in the cortex of the brain' (Portwood 1999, pp.5 and 11). When describing 'clumsiness' Barnett *et al.* say 'Medical evidence suggests that defects in the receiving and passing on of messages to and from the brain result in lack of co-ordination of eyesight and bodily movement, and sometimes cause speech disorders' (Barnett *et al.* 1989, p.50).

With regard to developmental verbal dyspraxia Rosenthal and McCabe comment:

> At one time people thought dyspraxia was caused by brain damage, but this has not been shown to be the case. The fact that it often occurs in several family members makes it unlikely for brain damage to be the usual cause. A very small number of children have dyspraxia as a result of other problems including galactosaemia [an adverse reaction to milk which can give rise to symptoms such as cataracts, visual impairment, gastro-intestinal disorders and jaundice], global developmental delay etc. but most are of an undetermined cause. (Rosenthal and McCabe 1999, p.3)

What does all this mean?

As there are usually no identifiable neurological signs to indicate dyspraxia, so the reasons given for the difficulties are all somewhat speculative. As mentioned in Chapter 1, it is thought that some dyspraxic children have difficulties with sensory integration. The child receives a variety of information through the senses – for example, from what she sees, hears, feels by touch or feels within her body in relation to gravity. She then has to integrate all these sensations in order to plan and carry out an action.

Young children learn many motor skills by cause and effect. For example, if they touch a toy hanging in their cot or pram something may happen. The toy may move or make a noise. This is initially an accidental response which becomes learned and subsequently relies upon the baby's ability to look and reach out with her hand and co-ordinate the acts of looking and reaching.

If a baby has difficulty in integrating the information received from her senses, then her ability to learn by cause and effect may be delayed.

CHAPTER 3

What are Children with Dyspraxia Like?

Boys are four times more likely to be affected by dyspraxia than girls. As the dyspraxic child is usually a boy, from now on we will refer to the child with dyspraxia as 'he'. In the first two sections of this chapter we will assume that the child being described is about six or seven years old, which is often the age at which he begins to experience real difficulties in school.

At home

As a baby he was slow at sitting, crawling and walking. Some dyspraxic children do not crawl. Some are slow at talking. As a schoolchild he takes ages to get dressed in the mornings. He cannot tie his laces and will not even consider trying. Even though he now has Velcro fastenings on his shoes he is reluctant to use them and tends to force his feet into the already fastened shoes that he shrugged off the night before. He sometimes gets them on the wrong feet and does not realise. He forgets to bring his reading book home from school. He cannot remember his homework. He is not sure on which day he has to take his PE kit. He always looks a mess when he comes home from school, with his clothes generally untidy, his shirt hanging out and his jumper sometimes inside out or back to front. He often has dirty hands and face. He tends to get into fights and disputes with other children over seemingly trivial issues. It is never his fault and people are 'not fair' to him.

He may have difficulties eating without making a mess. Cutlery can be a problem and his chewing may be 'messy'.

As he gets older and more familiar with the school timetable, he may complain of headaches or stomach aches on problem days – for example, PE day. He sometimes complains that music or household appliances are noisy. He still startles at loud noises. He may find that some textures of clothing irritate his skin.

In school

Handwriting and fine motor activities

In school the teacher is likely to notice that the dyspraxic child has poor handwriting and his work is generally untidy. He hardly ever has a pen or pencil available, and if he does his pencil needs sharpening. He often breaks it because he presses so hard when he is writing. His drawing is also messy, and not very recognisable. He may have great problems with the use of scissors, even 'special' ones. He never seems to be able to complete written work in time.

PE

He finds PE difficult. He finds it hard to throw and catch any sort of ball. He cannot skip, and finds kicking a football difficult. He sometimes makes odd compensatory movements with his hands and arms – for example, when running. 'Left' and 'right' often seem to be a problem when these terms are used. He also confuses positional words such as 'in front', 'behind' and 'beside'. He is always the last one to get picked when the children are choosing partners or teams. He often scorns an activity as 'easy', although when he tries he finds it very difficult – e.g. kicking a football accurately at a goal area.

He finds it hard to follow rules. Sometimes this is due to a total misunderstanding, as he has not listened carefully or understood the explanation given by the teacher. Sometimes he breaks the rules out of sheer frustration; for example, he never gets near the ball in a game of football and so he picks it up and takes it away.

He takes absolutely ages to get changed, both before and after PE. When the class has been swimming he may find it easier just to put his trousers on over his swimming trunks, or to take his trunks off and then 'forget' to put on his pants and even his socks.

Other classroom activities

He tends to be clumsy and to knock things over such as paint pots, and he scatters small maths equipment everywhere. He often bumps into other children when moving around the classroom or when running around the playground. The other children sometimes get annoyed about this. He always seems to be fidgeting and is unable to sit still. He cannot beat a rhythm in music, handles musical instruments awkwardly, and tends to play louder than the other children. He often forgets to bring his reading book and PE kit to school and frequently loses them.

He sometimes starts laughing and messing around during lessons when the children are supposed to be concentrating on written work. He usually finds someone willing to join him in this disruptive activity. At other times he does not seem to have many friends. When the teacher asks 'Who did that?' regarding a misdemeanour, the children usually say 'He did it' automatically.

He may have speech difficulties as well, which makes it difficult for his teacher and his classmates to understand him. He may get very frustrated when he is not understood or when his classmates mimic him or laugh at him. Sometimes he just cannot think of the word he wants to say and this may make him cross when other children answer for him. His difficulties in discriminating and sequencing phonic sounds may also affect his reading. Similarly, he finds it even more difficult putting his ideas into writing than putting his thoughts into words. He may have trouble with sequencing and time-related activities such as learning the days of the week, the months and the seasons and the concepts of before and after.

His general awkwardness with equipment and problems with positional words often mean that some numerical concepts pose difficulties for him. Completing maths worksheets can also be a problem because he finds it hard to form numerals and to carry out simple mapping activities which involve him drawing lines from one object to another.

His frustration at not being able to do things he wants to do, combined with low self-esteem, makes him irritable and prone to outbursts of temper. He may also be excitable and seem unable to sit still.

He will often find strategies for getting out of tasks that he finds difficult, such as writing. He may ask to go to the toilet or lose his equipment and ask to go and find it.

Moving to secondary school

Getting around

The child now finds himself in a much larger and more confusing environment. Instead of one teacher who knows him well he now has a number of teachers, some of whom he may see only once a week. Sometimes he is moving around the school with his form and can follow them, but at other times they may be split into sets and join up with other children. Sometimes the boys may go one way whilst the girls go another, as for example for sport or PE. He initially finds the geography of the school confusing. The time-table is another source of consternation, and he finds that hard to follow as well. Another major problem is organising his large, heavy school bag and carrying it around school. At lunch time he has to queue for his lunch, hold a tray and select and pay for his food whilst possibly still carrying his bag. There may be rules which he finds difficult to follow, such as keeping to the left or right of the corridor.

Writing

His writing was never very neat and it took him longer than most of the other children to finish things when he was at primary school, but now he finds it nearly impossible to write down the large amount of information expected of him at every lesson. He has to take notes when the teacher is talking, he has to copy information down from the board, and frequently at the end of the lesson the teacher quickly tells them to write down their home-work either from dictation or from the board. He finds that the others have gone before he has finished, and he either gets into trouble for taking so long or is late for his next lesson – providing he finds where he is meant to be going, that is. When he gets home and tries to read what he wrote under pressure of time, he finds it is illegible even to him and he cannot work out what homework he is meant to do.

PE and games

There seems to be more of an emphasis on team games at secondary school, and getting 'picked' is even more difficult especially as he still has problems catching, throwing, kicking and aiming. It sometimes seems to him a good idea to forget his PE kit and sit and watch. When he does have his kit he still finds he takes much longer than anyone else to get changed.

Practical lessons

New problems have emerged. He is expected to use science and technology equipment, and some of the things are quite hazardous. He still tends to knock things over, and this can be rather dangerous when he is cooking or using a Bunsen burner or woodworking or metalworking tools. He is usually paired by the teacher with someone who can do the task, and so tends to watch and give advice.

Paul: A case study

Paul[1] is nearly eight years old and attends his local primary school in rural Devon. He is the second of two children – his brother is

1   All the children's names have been replaced by pseudonyms in the interest of confidentiality.

two years older than him. The first concern his parents had was when they realised that his speech was delayed at about three and a half years old. He was speaking a few words but not very clearly, and he was not using sentences. His mother found this odd because he was developing well in other areas. Paul was a very happy child. He was like a whirlwind, charging around, banging and crashing into things and falling over. His family put this down to him being a big, boisterous boy. He clearly loved life and was very happy. He was obviously a bright child and his social skills were good. He interacted well from an early age with smiling and pointing, and had good eye contact. He had, however, shown an unusual lack of a sense of danger, and at 11 months had crawled up to the edge of a drop in a friend's garden and would have lowered himself off if he had not been stopped by his mother. It was clear that he would not have been able to manage the drop safely, but he himself was not aware of this[2].

As a baby he had never slept well and was always hard to settle; his parents did not have an unbroken night until he was three and a half. During the day he always napped well; he would tear around, tire himself out and then fall asleep. He also had some feeding problems. As a baby he would drink too much milk and vomit back a lot. When he started eating solid food he still had a big appetite but would often choke on his food.

As a young child he did not like loud noises and did not like getting water on his clothes.

Paul had shown very little interest in books. He would sit in bed with his mother with a book and turn the pages as fast as he could, then crawl across the floor and get another book. Then he would get back into bed and do the same thing again. He had never picked up on nursery rhymes or joined in saying the last words of familiar repetitive stories.

His favourite game was hide-and-seek. But he would always hide in full view, on the wrong side of the tree that was supposed to

2   Depth perception is normally present in babies as soon as they start to move independently (Dixon 1972; Gibson and Walk 1960)

be hiding him, and with his hands over his face. He would then be really excited when someone found him. He could never get the counting to ten at the beginning of the game right, either.

He had crawled at the usual time, and since he was obviously a bright child his family did not really worry until at his three and a half year old check it was clear that his speech was delayed. He was also still in nappies at this stage. He then had some speech and language therapy, but the speech and language therapist was quite reassuring and not over-anxious about his level of development. He went to playgroup before starting school, and loved it. His mother had noticed that if they started to sit at a table to do anything he was quickly off and playing with something else.

He then started school full-time, and within two weeks he was having temper tantrums and saying everything was too hard and that he could not do it. When the speech and language therapist went into school to explain about Paul's speech delay, she saw that he had other difficulties as well. Another speech and language therapist at the same centre assessed him and said that she thought he was dyspraxic.

Paul started school in January, and during his first term he refused to go. As soon as he was being dressed in his uniform he was taking it off again. His mother had to carry him to school to get him there. As the school is small both the reception and Year 1 children are in the same class, and so it was quite a structured class. The children spent quite a lot of time sitting at their desks, which Paul hated. He found he could not do the things he was being asked to do, like getting changed for PE.

The school asked the educational psychologist to visit, and a report was received by the end of Paul's second term. His parents had also requested that he be assessed at Vranch House, and he had this assessment shortly after the end of his second term. The statementing procedure took nearly a year, and Paul had extra classroom support during his second summer term when he was in Year 1. He had an hour a day initially but this has now been increased to about two and a half.

Once the school understood about Paul's difficulties and had advice and support the situation changed. His teacher's approach was much more flexible. She did not expect him to concentrate as long, she made allowances for him, and she praised him for good work.

When Paul was a toddler his mother had taken him to the local gym club, which he really enjoyed. There was a lot of free play and each child would have a very short individual session with the gym coach. When he was school age his mother took him back for two sessions but after that he refused to go any more. The sessions were now much more structured and he realised that he was unable to do the things the other children could do.

Paul has been attending groups at Vranch House for two years. At first it was the highlight of his week and he still enjoys coming. He has learned to swim and is now very confident in the pool. He has also improved skills such as jumping, kicking a ball, throwing and catching, and his fine motor control has improved.

He took the Key Stage 1 statutory assessment when he was seven and was assessed in all areas as working towards level 1. Now in school less than a year later, his maths is within the normal range although probably at the lower end of his age group. His reading has improved a lot in the last six months and he is learning words well and reading books with more text. His handwriting is still something that he finds difficult. Sometimes it is quite neat but at other times it is anything but. It is very hard for Paul to produce neat work every time.

In maths he sometimes mixes up the addition and multiplication signs. He is getting quite good at number patterns and maths games and the family play games at home which involve maths skills. They also play board games, dominoes and cards.

In the afternoons Paul's age group now go and visit the junior class to do activities such as art and science. His brother is in this older class. His mother says that Paul seems very capable now to people who are not familiar with his difficulties, and he is some-times asked to do things that are too hard for him. For instance, he was asked to do three activities as part of a planning exercise in the junior class. He had to draw a margin, put a title at the top of the page and do a piece of writing. He was quite upset that he could not do it.

The school recently had a workshop on dyspraxia for staff, organised by the Local Education Authority (LEA). The speech and language therapist still comes in weekly to see Paul and sets work for the classroom assistant to do with him.

One incident related by his mother shows Paul's determination to do things he finds difficult and demonstrates his growing self-confidence:

> They had a poetry day and the children had to take a poem in to class. In the afternoon when the parents were invited in, some of the children read their poems and Paul wasn't chosen. We had chosen a little football poem – four lines, which he'd been practising at home. When I went in he called me and said he hadn't been chosen to read his poem. At the end there was some time left and they asked who would like to read their poem. Paul had his hand up and they said he could read his.
>
> He was clattering around looking for this poem and his brother was looking too. There were my children – everyone else is sitting there, and they were clattering about trying to find his poem and David [his brother] was very concerned. Paul did eventually read his poem. He got up there and he read it – very badly. He had to be helped out, he obviously couldn't remember it, and he couldn't read it properly. He said to me afterwards 'They didn't pick me but I got to read it.' He was proud of himself. He's full of confidence. It's odd really, but he'll work quite hard to get into a situation where he probably knows he's going to struggle – but he really wanted to do that. He got there.

CHAPTER 4

How are Children with Dyspraxia Identified?

In most cases it is the parents who first wonder what is wrong, especially if the dyspraxic child is not their first. Things seem different and the child does not seem to progress at the rate they expect.

It may be when the health visitor checks developmental milestones that delays are noticed. The child may be behind on gross and fine motor targets, which are the first to be demonstrable. Later, the language milestones may be delayed. The child may walk without first crawling, or may have feeding and/or sleeping problems. He may also be 'difficult' and not easy to settle, or rather hyperactive.

If the child's difficulties are recognised at the pre-school stage either by the parents or the health visitor, then the parents will usually meet their general practitioner to discuss their concerns. Occasionally the nursery or playgroup may spot that the child is experiencing difficulties and mention this to the parents.

Following identification of a developmental disorder, the child may be referred to a paediatrician who may then refer him and his parents for specialist advice or placement at the local child development centre (CDC). Pre-school advisory teachers may provide advice and sometimes Portage workers may provide support in the home for parents. Portage is a scheme that originated in Portage, Wisconsin: a trained Portage worker suggests activities that a child with special needs can carry out with the help of his parents in his own home. Portage is only usually available for children who are experiencing a developmental delay of at least a year.

If the difficulties have *not* been picked up by the parent or the health visitor, then the school may notice problems when the child starts school. This may not come as a surprise to the parents, who may well have noticed differences well before their child started school. The school may find that the child falls over and bumps into things, is disorganised, is hopeless at getting changed, will not sit still and finds writing very difficult. Initially he may fit in, but find it very difficult when he moves from the more relaxed atmosphere of the nursery or reception class to join the Year 1 class. In Year 1 he is expected to pay attention, recognise routines and concentrate in group situations during the literacy and numeracy hours.

Having discovered that there is a problem, the school will follow the guidelines set out in the Code of Practice (Department for Education 1994a) involving parental consultation. (The Code of Practice will be described in more detail in Chapter 5.) It was produced following the 1993 Education Act to give practical guidance to Local Education Authorities and schools on assessing and helping children with special educational needs. After the school's initial assessment advice may be requested from the educational psychologist, the Social Services and the school medical officer, and via the school medical officer from health-related specialists such as paediatrician, physiotherapist, occupational therapist or speech and language therapist. Advisory teachers may also be involved – for example, those with expertise in information and communication technology or related special educational needs.

If the school has not taken action under the Code of Practice, parents who have concerns when the child is of school age can talk to his teacher, the special educational needs co-ordinator (SENCO) or the headteacher. A parent can request that the Local Education Authority carry out an assessment.

In some LEAs there may be a screening procedure at school entry which aims to identify children with delays in various areas of development. Dussart (1994) describes a screening procedure developed in East Kent to identify children with developmental co-ordination disorder (DCD) using a checklist completed by teachers which was followed up by using the Test of Motor Impairment (Stott *et al.* 1984). Portwood (1996) also developed a screening procedure in County Durham to identify children with dyspraxia. She asked teachers to screen the children using a number of criteria, and followed this up with a more detailed screening using the Wechsler Pre-school and Primary Scale of Intelligence, the Wechsler Intelligence Scale for Children (Wechsler 1990, 1992) and the Movement Assessment Battery for Children (Henderson and Sugden 1992). An intervention programme was then carried out.

As from September 1998 Baseline Assessment has been carried out with schoolchildren in their first half-term in a reception class There are a number of Baseline Assessment schemes used by different schools, all covering the following three areas: language and literacy, mathematics, and personal and social development. Some of the schemes also cover knowledge and understanding of the world, physical development and creative development. The aim of Baseline Assessment is twofold – to assess each individual child's abilities and from this to plan effective programmes of work, and to provide a baseline to measure progress as the child moves through the school. It is clear that some Baseline Assessment schemes are more able to identify motor difficulties than others. It would be helpful if, when they are reviewed, physical development could be included in all such schemes.

CHAPTER 5

How are Children with Dyspraxia Assessed?

In the previous chapter we discussed the identification of dyspraxia. Following identification, assessments may be made by various professionals. The route will be different depending on whether the child is in school or still of pre-school age.

Assessment at the pre-school stage

As already mentioned, the child's paediatrician may recommend that he visit the local child development centre (CDC), or alternatively he may refer him directly to another specialist. If the child is referred to the CDC, then the assessment will probably be carried out in a more informal way in a nursery setting. The CDCs normally have nursery teachers, nursery nurses, physiotherapists, speech and language therapists, occupational therapists, social workers and an educational psychologist either working at the centre or available to visit. If the professionals working with the child feel that his needs may be significant enough to necessitate a special school placement or extra provision when he reaches school age, then they will start the procedure described in the Code of Practice (Department for Education 1994a), which may eventually mean the child receives a statement of special educational needs.[1]

1   The Code of Practice is currently undergoing revision. It is expected to be in place and ready for implementation by September 2001.

Children in playgroups or nurseries may also be identified by the staff there as having special educational needs, and they too may inform the LEA after discussion with the parents.

However, it is unlikely that children with dyspraxia would be recommended for assessment under the Code of Practice for a statement of special educational needs at the pre-school stage. If a parent has concerns and her child is over two, she *may* ask the LEA to make a statutory assessment. The LEA then decides whether or not such an assessment is necessary. If they decide that it is *not* necessary they will write and tell the parents (in no more than six weeks) the reasons for their decision. Parents may appeal to the Special Educational Needs Tribunal if they disagree with the decision. Further details are given in the next section, 'Assessment at school age'.

The Department for Education publishes a very useful leaflet, *Special Educational Needs – a Guide for Parents* (Department for Education 1994b), which should be given to parents by the LEA if a statutory assessment is to be carried out. For details of how to obtain a copy see Appendix 1.

Assessment at school age

As mentioned previously, the child may be identified as having special educational needs by his school. The school must then carry out the procedures set out in the Code of Practice. For school-age children there are five stages of assessment. After stage 1, they may or may not progress through the other stages, depending on need.

Stage 1

At this point the school identifies that the child has special educational needs, gathers information and monitors his needs whilst attempting to meet them within the normal classroom situation. The concern about the child's special educational needs may come from a teacher, a parent or another professional such as a social worker or a health professional (e.g. school medical officer, speech and language therapist or physiotherapist).

Stage 2

The special educational needs co-ordinator (SENCO) becomes involved now that it is clear the child needs a more intensive intervention strategy. More formal advice is sought at this stage from professionals such as the school doctor or the child's general practitioner, education welfare officer or social worker. An Individual Education Plan (IEP) will then be drawn up by the school. This will list specific targets for the child to achieve and a date will be set to review his progress towards these targets.

Stage 3

At stage 3 the school decides it needs to call upon external support services to meet the pupil's needs. External support may come from an educational psychologist, from learning or behavioural support services, or from advisory teachers (visiting teachers who provide support in specific areas such as visual impairment, hearing impairment or specific learning difficulties). At this stage a further IEP will be drawn up which includes the involvement of external support services, and a review date will be set.

Stage 4

This is the stage when a statutory assessment of special educational needs is thought necessary, i.e. when the school considers that a statement of special educational needs will be needed. The LEA will be informed at this point. Formal advice will be sought from parents, from the educational psychologist, the school medical officer and other health professionals, the school, other educational advisory services involved and the Social Services. Before the final statement is signed the LEA will send parents a 'proposed statement'. They are asked to make any comments on the proposed statement and have only 15 days to do so. Parents can also ask for a meeting with the LEA to discuss the proposed statement.

Stage 5

This is when the final statement has been signed. The statement details the child's needs and the provision that will be made to address these needs. Next, the child's IEP will be reviewed and a review of his needs will be carried out every twelve months. Parents will be fully involved in annual review meetings, when the statement will be reviewed, the progress the child has made towards the objectives set will be discussed, and new targets set for the following year.

Assessments by specialists

Physiotherapy and occupational therapy assessment

The physiotherapist and the occupational therapist may be asked to assess children individually or as part of a multidisciplinary assessment – they may well carry out a joint assessment. Referrals may be made by the child's general practitioner, paediatrician or the school medical officer. In some parts of the country referrals may be made by educational psychologists, social workers or the headteacher. Referral procedures vary depending on the area, and there may well be waiting lists for assessment. These assessments may be carried out as part of the statutory assessment described above or as the result of a general concern expressed by the parents or by the medical practitioner.

Normally the physiotherapist will assess gross motor co-ordination. An assessment tool frequently used by physiotherapists is the Movement Assessment Battery for Children (Henderson and Sugden 1992), mentioned earlier.

The occupational therapist will assess fine motor co-ordination; this includes, depending on the age of the child, looking at his pencil skills with regard to writing or drawing. Other areas which may be assessed by the occupational therapist are visual-perceptual skills, tactile discrimination and daily-living skills such as dressing and eating, particularly if there are concerns in these areas.

The assessment may include standardised tests and qualitative observations. The therapist will complete a report following the assessment and suggest an appropriate plan of action. This plan may include individual or group therapy sessions, advice for the school and programmes to carry out in the home.

The physiotherapist may advise the school on activities for physical education which will help ensure that the child is included in PE as much as possible. Advice from the occupational therapist for the school may include pre-writing or handwriting exercises, recommendations on seating and on the positioning of writing (involving, for instance, a sloping board), and on drawing materials such as suitable pens or pencils or pencil grips. The therapist may advise on strategies to help the child master dressing skills; she may give a task analysis of a difficult skill such as tying laces. Advice may also be given on how to help the child overcome difficulties with eating meals – special non-slip mats or cutlery may be advised if necessary.

Speech and language therapy assessment

Speech and language therapists use a variety of standardised and non-standardised assessment tools. Information will be gathered from the parents regarding any feeding, swallowing, eating or drinking difficulties, as well as details about the child's understanding and his expressive language. From this information his developmental levels will be assessed. If appropriate, standardised assessments of receptive and expressive language will be carried out.

Other areas assessed by the speech and language therapist may include:

- Production of speech sounds and the sequencing of sounds including words in sentences

- Pragmatic skills (social communication) including the understanding of 'hidden meanings' (e.g. sarcasm, idioms, the importance of stress and intonation). The speech and language therapist may ask the parents and school to complete a questionnaire to help assess pragmatic skills

- Oral skills, which include the voluntary control of lips, tongue, jaw, the soft palate and other muscles of the mouth; and assessment of whether the child has a saliva-control problem. Also included is breath control as this affects speech – it may be 'breathy', or come in a rush – and quality of speech (e.g. whether the child's speech is too loud or too soft, the pitch of the voice and the intonation)

• Non-verbal methods of communication (e.g. the use of gesture, eye contact, facial expression).

The educational psychologist's assessment

Shapiro (1991) advises that 'before treatment is suggested, it is important for the child to have a full psychological assessment so that his particular cognitive pattern can be evaluated'. In most cases the child will be seen by the educational psychologist during stage 3 or 4 of the statutory assessment procedure described earlier in this chapter. This may take the form of standardised tests and/or qualitative observation and information gathered from teachers and parents. The child's performance with regard to the National Curriculum will also be taken into account, including any difficulties he has in accessing the curriculum (e.g. because of motor difficulties he may find it hard to record written work).

Portwood (1996, 1999), a senior educational psychologist, describes a series of assessments she has carried out to assess children with dyspraxia. Information collected would include background information on the family such as the number of children; the age of the mother; details of the pregnancy; birth details; the child's developmental profile including motor, social and language skills. The Wechsler Intelligence Scale for Children (WISC-III) (Wechsler 1992) would be carried out with children aged six years and older, along with a motor-skills screening test. With older children details would also be obtained of reading and spelling ages along with numeracy attainments and perceptual skills.

The WISC-III is a commonly used cognitive measure. Portwood says that often discrepancies between verbal and performance scores are used to diagnose dyspraxia, where the verbal score is significantly higher than the performance score. She considers that it is 'unhelpful to give the accumulative scores for verbal and performance IQ because that disguises the particular strengths in the child's cognitive profile' (Portwood 1998, p.14). The individual scores for the sub-tests which make up the two main sections – performance and verbal skills – should be viewed as a profile giving information on the child's abilities. The sub-tests which comprise the verbal scores give scores on information (general knowledge), similarities (why two words are similar), arithmetic, vocabulary, comprehension and digit span (repeating a series of numbers). The performance scores combine sub-test scores on picture completion, coding (copying symbols by drawing), picture arrangement (sequencing pictures in the correct order), block design (copying a two-dimensional pattern using cubes) and object assembly. Portwood considers that 'If the scaled scores in the sub-tests of arithmetic, digit span, coding and block design are significantly depressed in relation to the other scores, these are indications that the child is dyspraxic' (Portwood 1998, p.15).

The educational psychologist is often the professional who gathers all the evidence together from the various sources such as the parents, teachers and other professionals. She is instrumental in drawing up intervention strategies and co-ordinating them. The educational psychologist may offer specific advice on teaching programmes or be able to give parents information on support groups. She will also take the views of the child into account.

The class teacher's / SENCO's assessment

Nash-Wortham and Hunt (1997) give a simple method of assessment which can be carried out by teachers using six 'pointers'. These pointers do not assess whether or not a child has dyspraxia but give clear guidance on which areas he is experiencing difficulty. The six pointers are:

- timing and rhythm

- direction and goal (e.g. left, right, in relation to turning, pointing or movement)

- spatial orientation and movement

- sequencing (verbal and motor sequencing)

- fine motor control for speech, writing and reading

- laterality (whether a child has cross-laterality, i.e. mixed dominance such as being right-footed and left-handed).

Nash-Wortham and Hunt then give a series of exercises to address each of the six pointers. The exercises are clearly described and simple to carry out.

The assessment procedure used at Vranch House

It may be of interest to readers to hear of the procedure carried out at Vranch House Centre. School-aged children from the East Devon Health Authority area who have movement difficulties are referred to the centre for assessment and treatment. These children have a variety of movement difficulties due to cerebral palsy, muscular dystrophy, spina bifida, orthopaedic conditions or head injury as well as dyspraxia. On the whole, however, clinical conditions are usually identified at a much earlier age, and so a large proportion of the school-age children seen here exhibit dyspraxic-like movement difficulties.

Following referral a request will be made for a report from the child's present school. He will be assessed either by a physiotherapist or by an occupational therapist with an assistant. Where it is judged appropriate the physiotherapist and occupational therapist will carry out a joint assessment. The child and his parents will be invited for an appointment that will last about an hour and a half. Sometimes the child's learning support assistant from his school will be invited to attend, providing the parents agree. The family is made welcome and the assessment procedure is explained to them by the therapist. Initially the therapist will ask the child some simple questions to make him feel at home, such as his name, his school and what activities he does or does not enjoy.

The assessment includes some or all of the following procedures.

The Movement Assessment Battery for Children

As mentioned above, the Movement ABC is a commonly used assessment tool with children who have movement difficulties. It can be used for the assessment of children aged 4 to 12 years.

Test scores assess gross and fine motor skills in three areas:

- manual dexterity

- ball skills

- static and dynamic balance.

The test also involves:

- qualitative observations on the three above areas

- assessment of influences on performance (i.e. is the child observed to be overactive, passive, timid, tense, impulsive, distractible, disorganised or confused? does he overestimate or underestimate his own ability, lack persistence, get upset by failure, appear to get no pleasure from success?)

- assessment of physical factors (i.e. weight, height, weight in relation to height, vision, hearing, speech, anatomical or postural defects).

The test employs percentile scores. Children who score between the 5th and 15th percentile can be considered to have a degree of difficulty that is borderline. Opportunities for the practice of skills at school and home will be recommended. A score below the 5th percentile indicates that the child has a motor difficulty which requires intervention, such as a management or remediation programme. Scoring on or below the 5th percentile means that the child falls into the bottom 5 per cent of the population in terms of motor skills.

The Test of Visual-Perceptual Skills (non-motor) (TVPS)

The purpose of the TVPS is to determine a child's visual- perceptual strengths and weaknesses on the basis of non-motor visual-perceptual testing (Gardner 1982). Visual perception is the ability to use visual information to recognise, recall, discriminate and make meaning of what we see.

This test comprises seven areas of visual-perceptual skills; it shows how a child perceives various forms (black outline figures of two-dimentional abstract shapes, both familiar and unfamiliar) and the way these forms can be interpreted. The results indicate the likelihood of difficulties with schoolwork with regard to these areas, as follows:

VISUAL DISCRIMINATION

Difficulties with visual discrimination indicate that the child may have problems with the recognition of words, letters and numbers. He may find categorisation difficult, such as recognising similarities and differences in letter formation and patterns in the spelling of words. Matching words, pictures, letters, numbers and quantities of objects may cause difficulties too.

VISUAL MEMORY

Difficulties with visual memory may affect immediate and delayed recall of material when reading flashcards of letters, words and sentences, when reading words in books, and in remembering the form of letters when writing them.

VISUAL-SPATIAL RELATIONSHIPS

Difficulties with visual-spatial relationships may mean that the child has trouble writing words and letters on lines. He may reverse letters, numbers and words. Keeping neat margins and spacing between words and setting out maths problems may also be hard for him.

VISUAL FORM CONSTANCY

Difficulties with visual form constancy mean that it is more difficult to match letters and shapes and to recognise words out of a familiar context (e.g. if written in a different size, print or colour from usual).

VISUAL SEQUENTIAL MEMORY

Difficulties with visual sequential memory mean that the child may find it hard to sequence letters in a given order, which may lead to difficulties in reading and spelling.

VISUAL FIGURE-GROUND DISCRIMINATION

Difficulties in visual figure-ground discrimination mean that it is hard for him to see detail in pictures or text, and this may lead to difficulties in copying from the blackboard or from a written text or when transferring written material to a computer. The child may find it difficult to keep place when copying and so may miss out chunks of work.

VISUAL CLOSURE

Difficulties with visual closure can involve problems with recognising an individual letter, word or object from a partial presentation of its form. This will affect speed of accurate reading, the ability to study quickly a visual presentation such as a map or chart, and the ability to develop study skills in the older child such as speed- reading and scanning.

At Vranch House this test is used to give a profile of a child's performance within the seven areas of visual-perceptual skills. It is used to gain information on the areas of weakness which may have an influence on his handwriting abilities.

The Goodenough Draw-a-man Test

This test was developed by Florence Goodenough in 1926 and revised in 1963 to include three drawings that the child is asked to make – of a man, a woman and the child's drawing of himself (Harris 1963). The test can be used with children aged 4 to 12 years. It was originally designed as a measure of intelligence but at Vranch House it is used as a screening measure to evaluate conceptual maturity and to give an indication of intellectual functioning. This raw score needs to be used with caution because 9 out of the 50 items need lines to be 'firm and meeting' or 'attached' or 'continuous', and the ability to score on these items could be affected by motor difficulties which may or may not be related to intellectual functioning.

The Developmental Test of Visual-Motor Integration (VMI)

The VMI is appropriate for children aged 3 to 18 years (Beery 1989). Research has shown that the VMI used alongside other tests has predicted which children are likely to have reading difficulties. Predictive correlations decline as children get older, which is presumed to be due to their developing compensatory skills.

The test consists of the child using a pencil to copy a developmental sequence of 24 geometric forms. The ability to copy geometric forms is related to the skills needed in maths and handwriting. At Vranch House this test is used with children who have handwriting problems, with a view to advising on whether an individual's difficulties may be related to visual-motor integration.

Other observations of locomotor skills, posture, tone and stability

These aspects are observed during the assessment, and notes made. The other areas looked at include hopping, moving in a wheelbarrow position, stability in kneeling positions and strength in supine and prone positions. Locomotor skills such as walking on the heels and on different edges of the feet are observed, and any associated reactions with the hands noted.

Observations of handwriting or computer use

The child is asked to write his name, copy a simple phrase such as 'a big red bus' and individual letters and numerals. The writing is examined for the following points: consistency of the size of the letters, whether joined script is used, the slope of the letters, orientation to the line the child is writing on, and the spacing between letters and words. His hand and eye dominance is noted. Also observed is the type of grip the child uses to hold his pencil, and whether undue pressure is used. The therapist also notes his seating posture and the use of his non-dominant hand.

If computer use is being looked at, details are taken of the child's home or school equipment. His use of mouse, roller-ball or keyboard, and his seating position relative to the keyboard and screen are examined.

Other observations include asking the child to remember a short shopping list of articles and asking him to carry out a sequence of actions from memory.

After the assessment

After the assessment the child and the parents will be offered a soft drink and tea or coffee whilst the therapist looks at the test results. The therapist then discusses the results with the parents and gives some idea of what therapy or intervention might be appropriate and when it is likely to be implemented. A written report of the findings and recommendations is provided for parents and all relevant agencies. At the time of writing the criterion for a child to attend for regular therapy would be one of the following:

- The child falls below the 5th percentile in at least two of the three areas on the Movement ABC assessment.

- The child has scores on the Movement ABC between the 5th and 15th percentiles but also demonstrates a poor quality of movement from qualitative assessment.

- The child has significantly poor handwriting skills and there are concerns from school.

- The child has poor self-esteem, with some movement difficulty.

General considerations on assessments

The statementing procedure includes a multidisciplinary assessment. Assessments need to be carried out in a reasonably short time – children get tired if the session is too long. After the assessment, practical advice should be given. If a child is statemented then the Statement of Special Educational Needs should include advice and recommendations and be circulated to all relevant persons. The parents, the school, the therapists, the Social Services (if involved) and any other agencies involved, as well as the child, should know what has been recommended.

CHAPTER 6

Interventions in School

The class teacher's perspective

So a child in your class has been identified as having dyspraxia. You already knew he had special educational needs long before all the specialists were involved – in fact, you may have been the person to bring his difficulties to the attention of the SENCO and the parents. Depending on which stage of the Code of Practice he has been assessed to, you may or may not have a Statement. If you and your SENCO wrote his Individual Education Plan at stage 2, then you still may not be sure how to meet his movement needs as you have had no specialist advice. Alternatively you may have received reports with suggestions from the child's educational psychologist, physiotherapist, occupational therapist, speech and language therapist or other specialist support agency. They may have given you special programmes of work to carry out. The child may attend a special centre for therapy and you may have been given the name of a person to contact at that centre. It can be confusing and frustrating because you have many other children in the class with varying needs and the pressure of the literacy and numeracy hours, along with all the other initiatives that seem to arrive on your desk daily. You may have a couple of hours' learning-support-assistant time for the child if you are lucky.

I would advise class teachers to make sure they have the following documents or information:

- *Statement of Special Educational Needs* (if appropriate)
  Check that you have all the appendices as well. These
  are the detailed reports from the educational

psychologist, school medical officer and other agencies such as the Social Services. Parents' letters and submissions will also be included. The school medical officer's appendix may contain reports from a physiotherapist, a speech and language therapist, an occupational therapist or other medical specialists. The occupational therapist's report may be in the appendix from the Social Services, as many of them are employed as community occupational therapists and work directly for the local Social Services department alongside social workers. If a child has a care manager this person may be a social worker or a community occupational therapist. The appendices may not be with the final Statement because they are usually sent out with the proposed Statement, so you may have to request these from your SENCO or the Education Office.

- *Annual review reports* If the Statement is over a year old check to see you have these. If not, check with your SENCO.

- If the child does not have a Statement, check with your headteacher and SENCO to see if *any specialist reports* have been received from therapists, educational psychologists or others.

- The *names and telephone numbers of any therapists* currently working with the child – if you do not know who is involved the parents should be able to tell you, or telephone the centre the child attends and ask. Make sure you talk to the person concerned and invite him or her to come out and meet you at school.

- *The child's Individual Education Plan* If you were involved at stage 2 you should have this, but if the child has changed classes or even schools since stage 2, chase it up. Your SENCO should have it if you do not have a copy.

- Any *reports* from specialists that have been issued since the Statement. Check with your head and SENCO.

The parents' perspective

As parents you are likely to have been aware that there were difficulties long before the school mentioned it to you. You may have expressed your anxieties at an early stage in your child's development or education, and have had them brushed aside and been told that he is just 'a late developer'. You may have been instrumental in getting him a Statement of Special Educational Needs.

Make sure of the following points:

- If your child has a Statement of Special Educational Needs this should be subject to an annual review – i.e. the first one will be in a year's time. This will normally comprise the headteacher gathering reports from all relevant persons, including yourselves, and holding a meeting to which you and others are invited to review your child's Statement. Do check that this review happens – in some very small rural primary schools, when a child is the first there with a Statement, the headteacher may be unfamiliar with the procedure.

- Your child should have an Individual Education Plan if he has been assessed to at least stage 2 of the Code of Practice. This should be reviewed by the school regularly.

- Liaise with the school so that you can support the IEP targets at home where appropriate. Your child should also be aware of what targets he is working towards. They should be realistically achievable within, for example, a term or six months.

- Liaise with any other professionals providing support for your child – for example, the physiotherapist, the occupational therapist or speech and language therapist. If they are providing individual or group therapy sessions, be aware of what areas they are working on and make sure your child's school knows about this extra support.

- If your child receives extra time from a learning support assistant, find out her name. She may well be the person who gets to know your child best in school and who sees where problems develop before even the class teacher.

- If your child seems worried, unhappy or reluctant to go to school, talk to the class teacher. Remember – you know your child best.

Practical advice for the class teacher and learning support assistants

Handwriting and fine motor activities

Ensure that the child is sitting properly, as poor posture can have an enormous effect on handwriting or other fine motor skills. Even reading a book can be difficult if the child is wriggling around and has his head too close to or too far away from the book.

These are the basic points to bear in mind:

- The child should be sitting with his feet flat on the floor. His bottom should be well back on the seat and his overall posture should be symmetrical. His head should be in midline (i.e. in line with the centre of his body and symmetrical on his shoulders). He may find it much easier to write on a surface that is sloping slightly upwards. Special boards can be purchased or, alternatively, a large A4 file placed so that the spine is furthest away from him may well be sufficient.

- If the occupational therapist has advised on a special pen or pencil grip, ensure the child uses it. Special triangular pencils may also be advised, to encourage him to use a tripod grip.

- Check the child's pencil pressure. If he is pressing too hard his writing will be distorted and he will quickly become fatigued. Encourage a comfortable, effective pencil grip.

- The most appropriate paper position may not be square on the table but slightly angled.

- A labelled pencil case is a good idea, to keep his things together, as he may well mislay this item from time to time. Spares can be kept by his learning support assistant or teacher and returned to that person at the end of the lesson.

- Non-slip mats such as the Dycem range are a good idea for fixing all sorts of things to the table such as sorting trays, paint pots or exercise or reading books. These mats can be rinsed out quickly when they lose their power to stick and returned to their original condition. Dycem can also be bought in rolls and appropriate lengths can be cut off (see Appendix 1 for details).

- Soft plastic reusable adhesive putty such as Blu-Tack offers another useful way of fixing things, so make sure he has some in his pencil case.

- Handwriting practice sheets are helpful, as they give the child a model to start from and clear indications of where to start on the page. Having just a blank sheet of paper and being expected to copy off the black- or whiteboard may give him enormous difficulties. He may have to draw lines with a ruler first, and get them the right distance apart, before he can even work out where to start writing.

- Many children with movement difficulties find it easier to develop cursive handwriting rather than writing individual print-style letters. Many of the published handwriting schemes contain photocopy masters which encourage the development of flow in writing.

Rosemary Sassoon (1998, p.38) gives five essential rules of handwriting:

1. Our writing goes from left to right and top to bottom.

2. Each letter has a conventional point of entry and direction of stroke.

3. Letters have different heights.

4. Letters and words need to be spaced appropriately.

5. Capital letters and small letters are different and have different uses.

English and mathematics

One common problem is setting out work, particularly when writing or doing maths. Worksheets can be very helpful if they are simple and easy to follow. The aim of the maths lesson may, for example, be to practise addition of numbers over one hundred. Unfortunately, the child may spend most of the lesson setting out the problems, then adding the wrong numbers because the columns are not aligned. When writing, pre-lined paper may help.

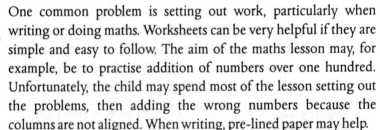

Another confusion experienced by dyspraxic children is that in reading and writing they are told to go from left to right, but in setting out mathematical problems they have to work from right to left. It is useful to discuss this with the children because they may never have realised the difference, and the awareness of this will help them to understand why they were getting it wrong.

Often, for young children the literacy and numeracy hours and other activities involve sitting on a carpet or on the floor. This is a difficult seating position for dyspraxic children, who may fidget a lot and become an irritation to their neighbours. If there is alternative seating such as classroom chairs, the difficulty may be overcome, although this has to be done sensitively so that the dyspraxic child is not singled out.

Physical education

This is one of the dyspraxic child's most challenging activities. If he manages to avoid physical activities because of fear of failure he will become less fit and the situation will get worse. O'Beirne, Larkin and Cable (1994) in a study of co-ordination problems and anaerobic performance found that children who were poorly co-ordinated were significantly less fit. Fitness is an issue in our schools at the present time because the modern child spends more time pursuing sedentary leisure activities such as watching television or playing computer games and at playstations. The suggestions here are specifically for the dyspraxic child, but will be useful for many other children with other special needs and for young children generally:

- Make sure all instructions are clear and simple, and that everyone hears them.

- If the children are in groups and going round a circuit in the playground, hall or gymnasium, be sure to provide a simpler alternative to any activities that are obviously going to be too difficult for the dyspraxic child. For instance:

    ° Ensure that climbing equipment has two routes, one higher and one much nearer the ground.

    ° With bat-and-ball activities ensure a range of equipment which includes lightweight large-headed bats with short handles, and larger foam balls.

    ° With aiming activities such as skittles or other target games, ensure that if balls are used, bean bags are also available. Larger targets will help as well.

- Make use of 'Beat you own record' activities. Children try to catch, bounce or jump more times in a minute than they did on the previous occasion. The use of the question, 'How many of you beat your own record?', offers a chance for the dyspraxic child to succeed even though his total may be lower than that of many other children. The learning support assistant can help him to count and keep a record if necessary.

- Circular non-slip mats or 'spots' are very helpful in a gymnastics lesson to help children to return to a 'space' in the hall or gymnasium. The action, by the whole class, of placing spots and then moving off and returning to a spot is a useful activity in itself. It also ensures that the dyspraxic child has a place to aim for and is not getting in anyone's way. Small gym mats are also useful in helping children stay in their own space.

- Non-competitive activities such as individual gymnastics or creative dance clearly give the dyspraxic child a better opportunity to work at his own level.

- When choosing teams in PE lessons it is clear that most dyspraxic children never have the opportunity to be leaders or captains. To circumvent this problem, teams can be chosen unconventionally. For example, the teacher says 'Everyone take a ball out of the basket', where there are, say, 12 yellow balls, 12 red balls, 1 blue and 1 green. The teams are formed by the teacher saying 'Everyone with a yellow ball go to the window end and everyone with a red ball go to the other end. The two people with blue and green balls come to me.' The latter two children are the captains or leaders for the next game. Obviously this particular method can only be used once, but there are many, many ways a creative teacher can sort the class into two teams without the children initially realising it.

- Rules should be explained clearly and repeated frequently.

- Use rhythmic speech where possible, with physical tasks. For example, all the children are standing in a circle and throwing and catching a beanbag around the circle. The teacher says 'To Robert' as she throws; Robert looks and chooses and says 'To Sally', and so on. In this way a rhythm can be established. The children are allowed to throw to their immediate neighbours if the circle is large. The use of rhythm in movement has long been thought to be beneficial to children with movement difficulties. 'Rhythmic intention' is a principle of the system of Conductive Education developed at the Peto Institute in Budapest for children with cerebral palsy.

A useful small booklet entitled *Special Needs Activities* describes activities for PE suitable for a wide range of children with movement difficulties (Knight 1992; see Appendix 1 for details).

Getting changed

This is another difficult area, as the dyspraxic child is often slow getting changed and may seem totally disorganised. Some useful tips:

- Have some sort of seating arrangement in the changing room, because it is easier to get changed sitting down and the dyspraxic child is less likely to fall over.

- Ensure that everyone puts the things they have taken off in a set place – for example, on a chair if they are changing in class, or in a bag or a locker.

- Ensure that everyone follows a school uniform labelling policy.

- Have someone check the changing area for missing items after each session. This may save a lot of time hunting for things later on.

- With younger children discuss the organisation of clothing as a lesson in itself. For example 'Put your clothes on your chair. Fold everything neatly. Put each item on the chair in the order you take it off. Put your shoes under the chair. Put your socks in your shoes.'

Art and craft

A lot of organisational skills are needed in art and craft. For example, if a child is painting he will possibly have paints either in pots or on a palette, and water for rinsing his brush along with his brush and paper. There may well be other children sitting round the same table and sharing equipment. So:

- Use non-spill water and paint pots.

- Ensure surfaces are protected by newspapers.

- Use painting overalls (these can be old shirts).

- Use non-slip mats – they are washable.

- If cutting out is a big problem for the dyspraxic child, the occupational therapist may recommend the use of special spring-loaded scissors (see Appendix 1 for details).

Music

It may well be difficult for the dyspraxic child to beat time, keep rhythm or play softly but the type of activities frequently practised during music lessons can be of enormous benefit in developing rhythm, listening and co-ordination skills. Again, many other children may well benefit from these activities, which might be suitable for a school lunchtime club. Here are some examples:

- *Clapping or tapping simple rhythms* These can be familiar rhythms such as those produced by tapping out the children's names, addresses, favourite bands or football teams. It can be done by clapping or tapping an instrument such as a wood block or a drum. When the children are familiar with the exercise they can tap their feet to the rhythm as an alternative. They all sit in a circle. To establish a rhythm, the first child taps her rhythm twice: for example, 'Jen-ny Smith, Jen-ny Smith'. Then the whole class joins in – 'Jen-ny Smith, Jen-ny Smith' – then the next child taps his rhythm, and so on.

- *Recognising name rhythms* The teacher claps a name rhythm, and if a child recognises her name in the rhythm she stands up (more than one child may have the same rhythm). The teacher carries on with the different rhythms until they are all standing up.

- *Action songs* These are good as warming-up or finishing-off exercises. There are lots of action songs that can be used with older children that are not babyish. Examples include 'Underneath the Spreading Chestnut Tree', 'The Hokey-Cokey', 'Heads, Shoulders, Knees and Toes'. Some suitable books of songs are given in Appendix 1. When doing action songs try to get 'quality' movement. For example, if a movement involves a stretch make sure it's a big one; or if they have to jump, talk about jumping correctly – 'Feet together, knees bend.' These bits can be practised before everyone sings the song. In the Hokey-Cokey, for example, the children have to distinguish between left and right; think which body part they are using; jump in and out with feet together; and do a stretch and a knee bend.

- *Starting and stopping* Using an instrument such as a drum, start a simple rhythm such as 'Walk, walk, walk, walk, Wait, wait, wait, wait', and repeat this several times. This activity can also be performed with the children doing 4 runs and 4 waits, with repeats. In a similar activity, the children move when the drum starts and stop when it stops. Encourage them to listen carefully and to be aware of having to balance when the beat stops. Alternatively, every time the music stops the children move back to their 'spots', as described in the section on PE (p.52).

- *'Join in the Game'* This simple song can be found in *Okki-tocki-unga* (see Appendix 1). Add a variety of actions – for example, 'Let everyone jump with me – jump, jump.' Everyone has to do the movement at the correct time in the song and to the correct rhythm. If the action is difficult such as skipping or hopping, then holding hands and doing the movement in a circle helps.

- *Playing loud and soft* The children play on musical instruments to a tune played on the piano or keyboard. Allow them to play as loud as they like as long as they go quiet when you tell them to. Play alternately loud and then soft, and repeat.

- *Playing and singing fast and slow* Learn a song at normal speed, and when the children know it really well get them to sing it or play along with an instrument really slowly, and then gradually speed up to very fast. This causes great hilarity but the children develop a real understanding of the effect of speed.

- *Producing vocal sounds* The children produce vocal sounds (e.g. ah, oo, ee, ae, mm) to a known tune, and change sound when directed by the teacher. The sound will change several times during the piece, so the children need to listen carefully.

- *Recognising instruments from the sound* The children have to recognise instruments they know well by their sound (e.g. drum, triangle, wood block, hand bells). The teacher hides behind a screen and one of the children either names the instrument or points to his choice from an array of instruments on the table.

When the child reaches secondary-school age

As noted in Chapter 3, when the dyspraxic child reaches secondary-school age he faces a lot of new challenges. For a start, he is in a much bigger school building. At the beginning of the day he has to go to registration, and he has to change rooms at the end of most lessons, carrying most of his books and equipment with him. There are lots of new faces, both adults and children, whereas at his last school he probably knew everybody. He also has to follow a written timetable. There may be new rules such as keeping to the left or right of the corridor when moving around the school. In the canteen or dining room he may have to queue for his lunch, carry a tray and pay for what he has selected. He may well have to catch a bus to school and then find it again at the end of the day, and at some rural schools there are large numbers of buses parked outside when it's time to go home.

The transfer

It is very important that transfer from the smaller primary school to the much larger secondary school is done sensitively. The primary SENCO will liaise with his or her secondary colleague about all the children who have special educational needs and discuss what special arrangements may have to be made. There will be opportunities for children to visit their prospective school during the summer term before starting in September. It is important that all teachers, not just the form teacher or SENCO, know what the individual children's difficulties are. Sometimes problems may have to be explained to other staff who come into contact with the children, such as the caretaker, and the office and canteen staff.

School bags

One of the biggest problems that the dyspraxic child faces when starting secondary school is the organisation and carrying around of his school bag. Nowadays in secondary school there are rarely any lockers, and the children have to carry extremely heavy bags around with them from lesson to lesson. There has been widespread concern about the health of children's and young people's backs, and parents have been encouraged to buy orthopaedically designed rucksacks, to be worn on both shoulders across the back. Unfortunately, the pupils rarely do this, and in the quick scramble from one lesson to the next they hook their bags over one shoulder. The young dyspraxic person is even less likely to be able to manage to put on a rucksack correctly. Added to this is the problem of organising the bag and bringing the correct items to school each day.

Following the timetable and keeping time

A written timetable can be very difficult for the dyspraxic child to follow. Colour-coding on the timetable can be helpful. The dyspraxic child may find it difficult to orientate himself around this large new building. He may well find that he is the last to leave the class, having spent longer packing his bag, and he does not know where to go to next as everyone else has disappeared.

Having a base to return to, in case of getting lost or experiencing general panic, is advisable for the new child. This may be the SENCO's room or the secretary's office where he can return and be pointed in the right direction.

The buddy system

Some schools use a 'buddy system' to help new children who may have difficulty in finding their way around their new school. An older child is asked to help that child initially and to generally 'look out' for him.

Physical education

As well as the considerations mentioned earlier in this chapter there are some particular problems regarding PE at secondary level. At this point team games become much more competitive, and any youngster who seems to be letting the side down by dropping the ball, not catching the ball or missing the football is made aware by the other children that his performance is not good enough and that he is not a welcome member of the team. If non-competitive options are available, they should be used. As mentioned previously, fitness is often a problem because as dyspraxic children get older they opt out of physical activity. The young dyspraxic person needs physical education even more than those who have no movement difficulties. Personal fitness programmes and activities such as swimming and trampolining can be based on an individual meeting personal targets – this will not only improve fitness and co-ordination but raise self-esteem as well.

Practical lessons

At secondary level lessons such as science and technology often involve using more sophisticated equipment than the young person will have used at primary school or at home. For example, using cookers, Bunsen burners, woodworking and metalworking equipment or sewing machines can be difficult and even dangerous for the dyspraxic pupil. He may even find unusual seating difficult, such as high laboratory stools. It is important that the individual subject teachers know the problems he is likely to have with equipment. These are lessons in which close supervision is essential and where the learning support assistant can be of invaluable help.

Recording work

For the young dyspraxic person recording work may still be a major problem. His handwriting may be more legible but is still likely to be slow and laboured. Taking down homework notes at the end of lessons is going to be difficult if these are quickly dictated or have to be copied from the blackboard. Small tape-recorders can be used for taking notes. Word-processing for homework should be considered as an option. If necessary, the use of a portable laptop computer should be allowed. Even this has its difficulties because the laptop is yet another heavy item to add to the school bag – and an expensive one if it is mislaid. Also, the pupil needs to know where he can print work out from his laptop. Photocopied notes prepared by the teacher are invaluable. Alternatively, a learning support assistant could make notes and photocopy them at the end of a lesson for any child in the class with special needs.

Reading maps, diagrams and music

These activities may well be difficult for the dyspraxic child as they involve interpreting abstract symbols and/or obtaining detail from a complex visual presentation. The use of simplified maps and diagrams will help – colour-coding is helpful here. Colour-coding can also be used when simple written music is being introduced.

Examinations

Consider in advance whether the dyspraxic child needs extra time or an amanuensis – a person such as a learning support assistant or teacher acting as a scribe – for examinations. For external exams these concessions have to be applied for well in advance and may require the support of a Statement of Special Educational Needs or other reports from the school or from other professionals.

Build up his confidence!

The child will become more independent as his confidence is built up. Success in itself builds confidence. Praise for good work and good effort should not be neglected, even if the targets achieved are small ones.

CHAPTER 7

How Can Parents Help Their Child?

Early days

Many parents develop a number of strategies through necessity and experience. Some good ideas suggested to me by parents of dyspraxic children are included in this chapter. There are many activities that can be carried out at home before the child goes to school.

Trust your instincts

The persons who know a child best are his parents. Many may be uneasy about their child's development, particularly if the dyspraxic child is not their first, but may be told by professionals such as health visitors and general practitioners that he is just a slow developer and a little delayed in his milestones.

Sophie's mother said 'She had her three-and-a-half-year check and I said to the doctor that I was really worried that she couldn't ride a bike. She was just pushing along with her feet. He said "Oh I'm not worried about that." You couldn't put your finger on what it was. We hadn't heard of dyspraxia or any sort of developmental delays or anything. My husband was really worried that she couldn't draw a person – other people at his work had two-year-olds who were drawing pictures of people. Everyone kept saying "Oh, she's fine".'

Emma's mother recalled that the health visitor had said 'Oh, she's all right, she's a late developer.' Emma's mother said 'When she was going to start school I said to the teacher "I don't think things are right. I can't teach her to write her name. She doesn't know how to spell", and she said "Oh, she's a late developer", and we had this for ages from the school. I kept being told "There's no problem", and I kept saying "Yes there is." You don't know who to get hold of, nobody seems to know anything about it.

'I took her to see the doctor because she kept falling over and asked if there was something wrong with her. He sent us to the orthopaedic hospital and they decided there wasn't anything wrong with her legs or her feet but they thought it might have been her eyesight because she has got a squint. She wasn't holding a pencil or anything in the right fashion and she used to scribble, and she wasn't making the same progress as Claire [older daughter] had made at the same age.'

Paul's mother said of the speech and language therapist 'I began to feel I was perhaps being seen as a sort of over-anxious, pushy parent. I was saying there must be some reason for his speech delay. I really thought she had got me down as somebody who expects their children to be reading. This was when he was three and a half and he was still in nappies. She sort of sat down with a sigh and said "Children develop differently". I know that, I do know that, but I felt that there was some reason for Paul having this speech problem.'

It is important for parents to realise that their child's progress *is* likely to be seen as delayed development, and the other problems displayed by dyspraxic children that the parents are aware of are not likely to be apparent in a clinical situation or on a home visit. With young children the difference between a small developmental delay and a more significant one is not very great. It is only as the child gets older and starts primary school that the differences become more apparent to those outside the home. So if a parent believes that there is a problem, he or she must not give up, but be persistent.

Eating and drinking

Many parents report early problems with feeding. Sophie had problems very early. 'When she was a month old she had to go into hospital because she was down to five pounds. Basically I didn't have enough milk. I think what had happened is that she was very fussy about latching on. The midwife kept coming round and watching me feed and said everything was fine. They left it too long, it was nearly four weeks. She seemed so content – she was really sleepy, she didn't cry and we didn't know she was hungry. We thought everything was fine. So then she started having bottles and she gained weight quite steadily. But when she was a year old that was when I really started to worry because she just seemed so undeveloped compared to all the other children. I remember taking her to her first birthday party and they were all moving around the room and eating biscuits. Sophie couldn't chew anything.'

As described in Chapter 3, Paul's problem was the opposite in that he would eat too much. 'He would prefer to eat with his hands, but since he's been at school we've been working on that. We've been working on eating and swallowing and slowing down and keeping his mouth closed when he eats and he's not so messy now. He is not to rush off and do something else until the meal is over. He still chokes a bit but not as much.'

Problems often continue as the child goes through school. Emma, aged nearly ten, still finds mealtimes difficult. Her father reports 'You see, usually in the morning after breakfast I wash up and usually Andrew [younger brother] wipes up. To get Emma to come out and wipe up was quite a job. I think she finds it difficult but recently she's come out and she's given a hand. She lays the table, not much trouble about that. She uses a knife and a fork but she drops no end of food, she's a messy eater.' Her mother says 'She still can't cut up. She can't hold and use her knife for cutting up. If she's not looking what she's doing she can quite easily tip the cup or glass. I daren't fill them very full – near the top and they'd be over.' Her father says that she wants to do things even though they are difficult for her, and will want to carry the drinks from the kitchen to the living room. 'I'll say about being careful with it and she'll usually get it to her mother without spilling it. She's a good trier.'

Getting the child to do these things is not always easy and there may be many spillages on the way, but clearly these are things that children *can* do as they mature, and they will be proud of being able to do household chores like their brothers and sisters.

There are many ways of helping a child to develop these skills:

- Use non-slip mats under plates and cups.

- Use larger-handled cutlery. An alternative is to put foam grips on normal cutlery.

- Don't fill cups and beakers to the top.

- Use plates and bowls with lips so that the food is less likely to end up on the table. Special plates, cups and cutlery can be obtained – if your child has an occupational therapist, she is the best person to ask. Alternatively, Nottingham Rehab produce a catalogue of items that can be purchased (see Appendix 1 for details).

- Ensure the child is seated properly at the table, ideally with feet flat and elbows at table height and with enough room on either side of him so that he does not interfere unknowingly with other family members.

- Whereas small children may wear a bib, this is not appropriate for older children, but they can use napkins tucked under their chin.

- Make sure all contents of packed lunches are easy to unwrap and easy to handle. With pre-packed yogurts it is difficult to remove the tops without the contents splashing over the person opening them. Carbonated drinks are likely to 'explode'. Crisp packets are often difficult to undo without the contents flying out. So put all drinks and foods into easy-opening containers. Put in easy-to-peel fruit such as bananas.

- Unsliced bread is a useful snack for children with chewing problems. This cannot be eaten quickly and forces the child to chew and exercise his jaw, lips and tongue muscles.

Sleeping

Some parents report that their children were unusually sleepy and contented babies, whereas others report difficulties with their babies settling and being erratic sleepers.

Paul's mother reported 'Paul never slept well, he was always hard to settle and we didn't have an unbroken night until he was three and a half. He always napped well during the day but he used to tear around and then he'd just flake out. When he was a baby that was for three or four hours. You see, I always had this ideal picture of Paul as an easy baby because he was just so happy all the time. So, yes, he did have sleeping difficulties but if he had been an unhappy child that would have been more of a problem.' Now at nearly eight years of age, 'his sleeping is much better than it's ever been, but it's not unknown for Paul to wake at half past four or come to our bed at half past five'.

If your child wakes during the night, then keep him as active as possible during the day and discourage naps. When he does wake reassure him, and then if he will not settle encourage him to do something quiet such as looking at a book, listening to a music tape or to a story through headphones. Have a nightlight in the room so that he does not feel frightened if he wakes. As he reaches school age he is not very likely to have the opportunity to nap during the day, so often the sleeping problems disappear.

Talking

Speech is often delayed with children with dyspraxia, although parents usually are not initially worried because the child usually has a good understanding of language. Sophie's mother reported: 'She seemed really bright, she seemed to understand everything but she didn't talk. She didn't start talking until she was way past three. At the nursery she went to, when she was nearly three and a half, they said I ought to think about seeing a speech and language therapist, and then that Easter she just started talking. She just came out with all these nursery rhymes and songs. They all came out from nowhere. I mean, she'd had odd words, and if she wanted something like a biscuit she'd just point at it and whine and whine. We'd spend half an hour getting her to say 'biscuit' and she just wouldn't. Looking back on it you'd say it's really stupid that I didn't realise, but I suppose it was because she was the first child. Sophie just seemed to understand. If you asked her to point to any part of her body she could do it and she could follow instructions.'

Emma also started talking late, but her parents put it down initially to the fact that her sister, Claire, who was nearly two years older used to talk for her. 'If you asked Emma a question Claire would always answer for her. We had this problem for ages. We kept saying "Let her answer for herself".'

Paul's speech was also delayed, and by the age of three and a half he was still only speaking a few words and they were not clear. His mother recalled 'I thought it was odd, his speech delay, because he was obviously a bright child and his social skills were good. He interacted well right from a very early age with smiling and pointing and eye contact. They were all extremely good so I thought this speech delay was odd as he was developing well in other areas.'

There are many activities that parents can carry out at home that will help to encourage language development. They are no different from those that any parent would carry out with non-dyspraxic children, but it is important not to abandon them because your child does not give a verbal response or loses interest in a short time. Try these:

- reading stories and looking at picture books

- saying and singing nursery rhymes

- playing games like 'Pat-a-cake', 'Round and round the garden', 'Peek-a-boo'

- repeating familiar stories, rhymes, songs and games –
the more often, the better.

Short and sweet and often is better than sessions that last a long time and become a battle to keep your child's attention. Stop as soon as he loses concentration.

Crawling and walking

Children with dyspraxia often walk late and may not crawl or may have unusual crawling patterns.

Lisa did not walk until she was 19 months, and her mother said she realised that although this was not unusually late 'she didn't seem to be very strong with it. She was very late pushing up on her hands, on her front palms and that sort of thing.'

Sophie walked at the same age but did not crawl. Her mother recalled that at a birthday party with other children 'she used to sit on the spot and she couldn't reach the toys and then she'd just give up. My friend had a baby-bouncer and we put her in and she just pulled her legs up, she wouldn't touch the floor. She never pulled herself up to walk round the furniture. She never crawled, and then she started bottom-shuffling and she would even bottom-shuffle through a tunnel and she'd go really, really quickly. She would do a lot of hand-flapping. One day when she was nineteen months she very, very shakily stood up and stumbled across the room and then she started walking.'

On the other hand Emma walked early, at ten months. 'She didn't crawl very much but when she did she always went backwards and not forwards.'

There are a number of resources that can be used to help the pre-school child improve his motor skills. 'Tumble Tots' (a gym club for young children) and a toddlers' gym club are resources that parents have used in East Devon. There are also private play areas specially for toddlers, which have soft play areas, ball pools and appropriate toys. The best way to find out what is available locally is to ask your child's occupational therapist or physiotherapist, the staff at playgroup or nursery, the pre-school advisory teacher or other parents. If all else fails try the local library, civic centre or town hall, or *Yellow Pages*.

Sensory awareness

Dyspraxic children can show an oversensitivity to sensory stimulation, whether in response to noise or to tactile stimuli.

NOISE SENSITIVITY

Paul's mother recalled that, although he was a very confident child and not likely to be upset by anything, 'Once getting out of the car at a friend's house, the children in the house were upstairs banging on the window but we couldn't see them. Paul was really scared and he couldn't see what was making the noise. It wasn't particularly loud. It didn't make me jump. He will say now about the radio or music "It's giving me a headache."'

Sophie's mother said 'From a very young age certain toys made her hysterical and upset. She had a little doggie and when it barked she used to really cry and cry. She had a musical doll that my husband's parents had given her and they had to hide it away because she got so distressed. (It is smell as well, certain smells she can't stand.) I always remember when I sat in on the first group she went to at Vranch, it was really funny – it was quite a relief as well. The children were all sitting in the hall and somebody moved a chair on the other side of a screen, and about five of them turned round and said "What was that?" It was in stereo, all five of them at the same time.'

As an older child Emma still does not like school discos – she tells her parents 'It's too noisy and I don't like the lights.'

Lisa was also sensitive to noise when she was a baby. Her mother said 'She absolutely hated me using the vacuum cleaner until she was about two. At that age we bought her a toy vacuum cleaner and that really helped her to overcome it. We also moved to a slightly bigger house which meant I could put her at one end and start vacuuming the other end. As a small baby things like a lorry going past on the road would make her cry and she still has an incredible sensitivity to alarms. We have a burglar alarm and a smoke alarm and even when you set the alarm you can see her slightly tensing up just because it beeps. She's used to it now, which is good, but one night the smoke alarm malfunctioned – there was no fire or smoke or anything and it wasn't even making the noise it was meant to make. It was just making a high-pitched whistle. For about a week afterwards she couldn't sleep in her own bed, she was so upset by it and so worried about it going off again. She is very, very sensitive to certain noises but not to noise overall.'

TACTILE SENSITIVITY

Paul was sensitive to things on his skin. His mother said that as a pre-school child he didn't like water getting on his clothing and making it wet. Emma's parents found that as a baby she reacted when the car started moving, 'You know, when you put a child in the car it usually sends them to sleep. When we put Emma in the car as soon as it started she would bawl, she went on for ages. She was never sick but as soon as the car started moving she'd start crying.'

DEPTH PERCEPTION

Paul's mother also recalls how he was not sensitive *enough* to certain visuomotor stimuli, 'I remember once when he was crawling. He was only about eleven months or so and we were in a friend's garden which was a sort of terraced lawn but with quite a drop. I was watching him and he crawled right up to the edge of this drop. He looked over and studied it and he was about to lower himself off. There was no way he could manage that drop. I thought that was odd because young babies don't do that, they have depth perception.' (See also note on p.24.)

The schoolchild

First days at school

Starting school may be a difficult time, especially as nowadays reception classes are often more formal than they used to be even five years ago, with more structured literacy and numeracy activities. Often the dyspraxic child has loved nursery or playgroup and enjoyed the freedom of being able to go from one activity to the next without having to sit down, be still and listen for more than a short while.

Paul had loved his playgroup, but within two weeks of starting full-time at school things were clearly wrong. 'He was terrible and was having temper tantrums. He had never been a child with this kind of problem. He was saying "It's too hard, I can't do it, it's too hard." The first half-term was difficult as he didn't want to go to school. He was a school refuser, actually. It made me realise how difficult it is if you have a child who is refusing to go, because it's really hard to get them there. He was taking his uniform off as fast as I was getting it on. I had to carry him to get him to school, so it was very traumatic. It was really awful the first few weeks, but I think he had quite a hard time because it was quite a structured first class. The teacher has them in her class for two years and she has them all reading. They spend a lot of time sitting at desks, which Paul hated. He couldn't do all these tasks they were asking him to do, things like getting changed for PE.'

The important thing is for parents to talk to the class teacher about any problems their child is experiencing as soon as they become apparent. The parents of a dyspraxic child should make the school aware of any difficulties before the child starts school, so as to alert the teacher to the fact that sitting still for long periods may be difficult and to raise awareness of those difficulties described in Chapter 6.

Dressing

The dyspraxic child is likely to struggle with getting ready for school in the mornings when everyone is busy and time is limited. As noted earlier, getting changed before and after PE or swimming, putting coats on and taking them off at the beginning and end of school and playtimes are also difficult.

SOPHIE, AGED 7

'She gets undressed. She's got Velcro shoes. She's a lot better, she can put her socks on now. She's got this thing that she can't do her shoes up tightly enough. She always says "It's not tight enough" and that drives us mad. She always has to ask which way round her knickers go and which way round her vest goes. When she comes home she's always really tired and she can't manage to get her sweatshirt off very well. She can do buttons now but she cannot do jeans buttons and zips. We haven't really attempted laces yet.'

LISA, AGED 9

'She still gets in a hopeless muddle if her clothes are inside out. She tends to cast them off, just in a heap, before she goes to bed. I make sure they are all the right way round for the next morning and that the last thing she has to put on is at the bottom of the pile and then she can work down the pile. She takes a terrific amount of organising. Every day she will come out of school minus something or other that she needs for the evening, and often with her shoes on the wrong feet. That's absolutely classic, really isn't it? Her buckles are half undone and her tights are inside out. She's always a little bit muddled. It does take her longer. She asks for help wherever she can. With doing up shoes she's always very reluctant to spend the time to persevere and do it herself. She'd rather just ask someone else to do it for her. It's always difficult striking a balance. On the one hand you feel it's really good for her to have as much practice as she can, but then she gets so frustrated.'

EMMA, AGED 10

'She cannot do things like tying up shoelaces, she has difficulty with buttons and left and right. I leave little markers to show which shoe goes on which foot. Sometimes she has got things on back to front. You tend to buy shoes and clothes that you know she's not going to have too much difficulty getting on and she'll be able to find the right way so that then she is more independent. Sometimes she does not know which way her shoes or clothing go and she has to ask, which she finds frustrating. She used to have problems doing up shoes, you know, buckles as well. She mastered buckles about three years ago. It took her ages to get the thing in the right holes. Gloves or mittens are another thing she has problems with. With gloves she can never work out which finger goes in which hole. You sort of get two or three fingers together. There are some mittens that she can never seem to get the thumb in so she's usually thumbless. She doesn't like mittens very much.'

There are lots of ploys that parents use to help their children with dressing – some of the main ones are listed below:

- *Label all clothes* All children lose their clothes at school from time to time but the dyspraxic child is likely to do this more often than most, so ensure that all clothes are labelled with your child's name.

- *Label his shoes 'left' and 'right'* Shoes can be marked 'left' and 'right'. Some people use the letters L and R and some use colours such as red and green. The origins of using red for left and green for right can be quite interesting for a child and might fire his imagination. The nautical use of green for right (starboard) and red for left (port) in lights for boats, ships and aeroplanes can be seen if you live near the sea or an airport. The old nautical saying, 'The captain *left* his *red port* wine behind', might also intrigue your child. Of course, it does not help if he still has difficulty in remembering which side *left* is. Another aide-memoire is to tell the child to hold his hands in front of him, palms downwards with the thumbs out – in this position the left hand makes the shape of a capital L. One solution might be to use a red capital L in left shoes and a green capital R in right shoes. Another useful tip *for right-handed children only* is to say 'I *write* with my *right* hand.'

- *Use Velcro fastening* This method of fastening can be used on all sorts of clothing. Nowadays shoes for both

children and adults commonly have Velcro fastenings.
Jackets often incorporate both zips and Velcro. Velcro is
easier and quicker than laces and zips and buttons.

- *Distinguish front from back* Another difficulty is knowing
  which is the front and which is the back of a jumper or
  other item of clothing. Point out to your child that a
  label is always at the back. In addition, having a
  distinctive pattern on the front often helps.

- *Make sure that garments are large enough* All children have
  experienced times when their head and ears are stuck in
  the neck of their jumper. Make sure this does not
  happen by ensuring that your child's clothes are
  reasonably loose and easy to pull on and off. If they are
  too big, however, he will find sleeves that are too long a
  distraction and a nuisance.

- *Use elastic in waists and with buttons* Elastic-waisted skirts
  and trousers make things much easier. Often school
  uniforms nowadays are much easier to take on and off,
  with T-shirts, polo shirts, sweatshirts and jogging pants
  being quite common. Adding loops of elastic to button
  holes can often help to make fastening easier. Fastening
  gloves to each other with elastic and threading it
  through armholes may be practical and helpful with the
  very young, but is frowned upon by most children of
  school age as babyish and consequently may cause more
  problems than it solves. Adaptations to clothing have to
  be done sensitively, as today's children are often very
  definite from quite a young age about what they find
  acceptable to wear.

- *Sort out his swimming kit* Getting tight-fitting swimming
  costumes on and off can be a nightmare, so ensure that
  costumes and trunks are easy to put on and remove.
  Having a distinctive towel is useful, so that your child
  knows at a glance which is his. A swimming bag should

be large enough to get the towel in *after* it has been used and is no longer neatly folded. Include a plastic carrier bag to put the wet costume in as soon as it is taken off so that the dry clothes do not get wet.

- *Choose a sensible school bag* School bags should be practical – not too big, but large enough for your child's purpose at the stage of schooling he is at. A distinctive style is helpful, so that he recognises his bag quickly. Often primary schools nowadays have uniform school bags, which makes it more difficult. If the school permits, use stickers to make the bag more easily recognisable.

- *Check loops on coats* Many young children have difficulty in hanging their coats on hooks because the loop inside the collar is too small for them to be able to manage it. Making a bigger loop will not only ensure that the child achieves this task but will also mean that the coat is not lying on the floor all day – possibly getting trampled on by passing feet.

Organising

Initially you will be organising your child's day and remembering things such as the school bag and the packed lunch, and you will be aware of his timetable. Most parents find it helpful to start involving children in this organisation as soon as possible – to go through questions such as 'What day is it tomorrow? What lessons do you have tomorrow? Have you got your reading book, home-work, swimming things?' Gradually the child will begin to take responsibility for this, but will have benefited from having had a routine built up by his parents. Every evening, encourage him to think which day it is tomorrow, what he will need and whether he has the routine things he needs every day, such as his packed lunch. Pictorial lists or timetables will help. These can be hand-drawn, or use pictures cut out of magazines.

Home exercise and speech programmes, and homework

Try and make this time fun and special for your child. Do not involve brothers and sisters in the exercises, as they will undoubtedly do better. Make it your special time with your child.

Remind him about his homework. Talk to the school if problems seem to be developing. If his homework takes him an inordinate amount of time compared to other children, let the school know.

Encourage his leisure activities

It is important for children as they get older to develop leisure activities and hobbies. If a child has a real interest in an activity he will become enthusiastic and achieve levels that may seem unlikely at first. Fitness is of particular importance because, as mentioned earlier, children who are not very able at physical activities tend to avoid them and become less fit. Generally non-competitive sports should be encouraged, such as swimming, horse riding, trampolining and bicycle riding. All these activities are good for developing co-ordination and fitness as well as being enjoyable. Some children do develop interests in sports which *are* difficult, but through perseverance they often manage to achieve success. Parents' reports of children with dyspraxia mention one individual who had become a member of the school football team and another who enjoyed ballet and tap lessons.

Small-scale apparatus in the garden can help your child develop skills in a protected, non-competitive environment. Swings, slides, climbing frames and trampettes (small trampolines) can all be purchased for home use. Regularly following home exercise programmes set by the physiotherapist can also make a big difference. A new home therapy programme used by Vranch House is the Pindora's Box programme developed at Pinderfields Hospital (Pinderfields and Pontefract Hospitals NHS Trust 1999). It is designed to help in the training of fine and gross motor skills with children aged five to ten years old. There are five levels. The therapist goes through the programme with the parents, who then take home the programme and equipment needed to carry it out. Each level contains eight exercises which consist of gross motor and fine motor exercises and a rhythm-based activity. Each level takes about twenty-five minutes to run through the first time, but the time taken decreases as the child becomes familiar with the activities. The therapist gives the parents the programme and equipment needed for two weeks. During this time they go through all activities eight times (or at least six).

Regarding home activities, Paul's mother said 'What we found he really liked and I think is really helpful are all sorts of board games, dominoes and playing cards. We are teaching him to play bridge. He's really interested in it and very motivated and it has a lot of skills. You have to be able to count the points, to remember what's gone and to take turns. So we do a lot of those games.'

Many children also develop an interest in computer games. Often the standard mouse is difficult for them to control at first, especially using the drag-and-point facility. There are a number of types of children's mouse or roller-balls available, which they often find easier initially (see Appendix 1 for details).

Relationships with other children

Often the dyspraxic child has difficulties in developing friend-ships. He or she may tend to play more with younger children. Lisa's mother reported 'She has never really had a close friendship that has lasted. She likes younger children who she can mother and she likes older children who will mother *her*, but it's quite difficult for her to have an equal relationship with a child of her own age.' Often the child develops a close friendship with another child who has similar difficulties, and this may well turn out to be a long-lasting relationship.

Give him credit for effort!

Parents know that their child often works very hard but gets very little credit for it. A dyspraxic child often has to put out an enormous amount of effort to do something that another child can do easily. He will often be very tired at the end of the day.

Praise is a great motivator, and it is important to give credit for effort expended along the way rather than just for the end result.

CHAPTER 8

Therapeutic Interventions

Physiotherapy and occupational therapy

Research

It is difficult to prove whether a long-term programme of therapy has benefited a group of children or not because it is impossible to know what their progress would have been like without the intervention. But there have been a number of intervention programmes described here that would indicate that children *do* benefit. Williams, Smith and Ainsley (1999) carried out a study with a group of 15 children with developmental co-ordination problems. The children were assessed using the Movement ABC before and after a ten-week intervention programme and were found to have shown improvement in overall performance, particularly with ball-related skills. The intervention programme consisted of a forty-five-minute session once a week, supported by a home exercise programme. In the first stage of a long-term study Losse *et al.* (1991) found that when the children designated as 'clumsy' took part in a year-long intervention programme, many of them made significant progress in the area of learning motor skills.

Common sense would lead us to believe that if we find certain skills difficult and we practise them regularly, they are likely to improve. If we do not practise them or even actively avoid doing them they may become worse, and certainly an individuals' confidence in carrying out these skills will diminish.

The North Devon Children's Physio Department carried out a survey to examine the effectiveness of therapeutic intervention with regard to the children with dyspraxia (Sylvester 1999).

Questionnaires were sent to referrers, teachers, parents and children in respect of 41 children who had received physio treatment in the preceding twelve months. Ninety-four per cent of respondents said that the report, advice or intervention received had added to their understanding of the dyspraxic child's difficulties. Improvements were seen in the areas of handwriting, self-esteem and PE by over 70 per cent of the respondents.

Individual therapy

In some areas of the country the child may be offered individual therapy sessions over a period of time. The therapist may also give a home exercise programme for parents to practise with their child, and may give advice to his school on how to plan activities for him in PE lessons.

Group therapy

Group sessions may be offered at a specialist centre, or at the child's school if there is a large enough group of children who would benefit from such sessions. Usually groups are small – no more than eight children. Again, the therapist may offer home exercise programmes and advice to the school on PE.

Activities

Group and individual sessions will focus on a number of areas.

GROSS MOTOR SKILLS

Ball skills

- Activities such as catching, throwing, rolling, aiming and kicking, using a variety of balls and beanbags, as appropriate.

Balance and co-ordination

- Activities such as walking, running, hopping, skipping, jumping, cycling

- following different tracks or patterns on the floor

- walking, running or cycling along a slalom course, using cones

- using ropes for skipping and jumping

- changing direction during a movement and maintaining balance

- maintaining a balance when stopping or when in a held position

- balancing in various positions such as on one leg, in a squat position, from all fours, and lifting different combinations of arms and legs

- moving forwards, backwards and sideways

- sideways and forwards rolling.

Swimming

Swimming is particularly helpful for children with co-ordination difficulties because they have the support of the water when they are moving in the pool. Therapeutic swimming programmes such as the Halliwick method involve the children in the following activities:

- developing breath control by learning to blow out in the water

- learning to walk, jump and move in a controlled manner in the pool

- learning to enter the water safely from the side

- developing a controlled float and maintaining stillness in the water

- becoming safe in the water by developing swimming skills.

Figure 8.1: Floating in the pool is relaxing.

The Halliwick method was established in 1949 by James McMillan at the Halliwick School for Girls in London. The children are taught swimming on a one-to-one basis but within a group-based activity. The Halliwick Association of Swimming Therapy arranges courses to train instructors in the methodology and will know where Halliwick swimming is taught in an area (see Appendix 2 for contact address).

Trampolining / rebound therapy

Working individually with the therapist, the dyspraxic child discovers the many benefits of trampolining, or rebound therapy. The general benefits are that the limbs become stronger, and muscle tone improves along with stamina and general co-ordination. Other specific benefits are improvement in reaction speed, in spatial awareness and in body awareness, and improved height and depth perception.

Figure 8.2: Blowing plastic eggs across the pool helps to develop breath control.

Figure 8.3: Having fun in the pool.

Figure 8.4: Side stepping.

FINE MOTOR SKILLS

If physiotherapist and occupational therapist are working as a team, then this area is more usually covered by the occupational therapist.

Hand function

Activities may include painting and drawing exercises, craft activities and cooking, as well as simple exercises to improve hand function.

Daily-living skills

The therapist will usually provide help and guidance with mealtime skills, including the use of cutlery; dressing skills; toiletting skills; seating and general posture. Normally she will advise parents on improving these skills and on any suitable equipment that might be needed.

Figure 8.5: Jumping sideways.

Figure 8.6: Moving to a rhythm.

The therapist may also visit the school and advise on these areas if necessary.

Handwriting

The therapist will recommend suitable writing equipment, seating position, posture and pencil control. Activities will include pencil and pen exercises involving tracking from left to right, making up and down strokes, and developing flow by doing a series of writing patterns. She will not usually work on set writing schemes because, if the child is working in a group, all the children may be from different schools, which will have different writing schemes. The skills worked on will be those that will help the child to develop the skills he will need whichever writing scheme he is using.

Speech and language therapy

Speech and language therapy may be delivered individually or in a small group. It may be offered at a centre or carried out at the child's school. The speech and language therapist will also offer advice on home programmes. She may give the special support assistant programmes of work to carry out in school. She may also give advice if the child has difficulties with eating or saliva control.

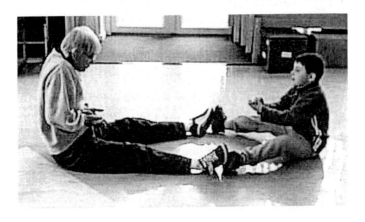

Figure 8.7: Throwing and catching a beanbag.

Activities

- Motor skill training, which involves speech movements and sounds; sometimes movement exercises are done before speech is practised. The Nuffield Programme uses this type of approach (Connery *et al.* 1992)

- Activities for developing pragmatic communication skills (i.e. social communication)

- Activities for developing receptive and expressive language

- In some cases signing may be recommended to support developing speech; Makaton signing is often used (Walker 1976)[1]

---

1   Makaton signing is a simplified version of British sign language, with a small core vocabulary of about 350 language concepts. Key signs only are signed along with normal grammatical speech.

- For some children with limited speech augmentative communication systems might be recommended, using pictures or symbols and/or voice-output communication aids. Examples of picture and symbol systems are Makaton symbols (Grove and Walker 1990); Blissymbolics (Hehner 1980); Picture Communication symbols (Mayer-Johnson 1989) and Rebus symbols (Clark, Davies and Woodcock 1974). These systems are usually only recommended if speech is very limited; while encouraging the development and use of speech they also provide the child with a communication system to use both at home and in school. Voice-output communication aids may be recommended when the child's speech is very limited. These are devices that he can use to 'speak' by using a keyboard, touchscreen, mouse or switches. They can be pre-programmed to give him access to the words he is most likely to need, or he can type words directly on the keyboard which will then be 'spoken'. An example is the DynaMyte augmentative communication device (see Appendix 1).

Vranch House Centre

It may be of interest to the reader to read of the work done at Vranch House Centre. The work here differs from that of many other centres in that the children receive their therapy mainly in groups. This means that many more can be seen and that they have the benefit of working with other children with similar difficulties. The group dynamic also has a positive effect in encouraging the children to work co-operatively, to learn to take turns and to develop listening and observational skills. The assessment procedure used at Vranch House has been described in Chapter 5. Also detailed there were the criteria a child needs to fulfil in order to attend for regular therapy. After this assessment, he may be offered one or more of the following.

Individual therapy sessions

Individual physiotherapy or occupational therapy sessions may be offered at Vranch House.

Regular weekly therapy groups
BASED AT VRANCH HOUSE

Group therapy may include swimming, PE skills, handwriting, craft activities and co-operative games. The swimming and therapy groups take children from approximately 5 to 12 years of age in small groups of up to ten. There is a progressive route within the programme and the children move from one group to another. The children in these groups come weekly for two hours, and attend a swimming session and either a fine or a gross motor group, depending on the individual child's need.

There are two other groups, of which one comes to improve handwriting skills for an hour a week and the other, a younger group, comes for PE and fine motor skills.

Figure 8.8: Crumbling biscuits to make cakes.

Figure 8.9: Decorating cakes.

AT EXETER GYM CLUB

Activities include trampolining and rebound therapy, gymnastics skills and co-operative games. These sessions are usually offered to younger children who live in the Exeter area and can attend a lunchtime session at the Gym Club. This group often acts as a feeder group before a child starts attending a group at Vranch House.

AT 'TIGGERS', CLIFTON HILL SPORTS CENTRE, EXETER

This after-school group is run by a coach from the Sports Centre under the direction and supervision of the Vranch House therapy team. The children participate in trampolining, ball-skill practice and team games. These sessions are usually offered to children who are borderline or too able to need regular therapy but whose parents are keen for them to improve their physical skills. Children on the waiting lists for group sessions at Vranch House may also be offered these sessions.

AT ST LUKE'S CAMPUS, UNIVERSITY OF EXETER

The children are paired with sports science students from Exeter University and work on individual programmes, co-operative games and swimming. Activities also include trampolining and the use of multigym equipment. One group consists of older children who have worked their way up through the Vranch House groups and take part in both PE and swimming and have the advantage of using the full-size swimming pool at St Luke's Campus. Another group of older children who have been more recently assessed take part in a PE session.

Figure 8.10: Trampolining improves co-ordination.

Holiday activities

When a child has successfully completed the weekly swimming and therapy programmes he may progress to the holiday programmes which run in the Easter and summer holidays. Some older children also have holiday provision, as well as receiving regular therapy. Holiday activities may take the form of:

- handwriting workshops
- sports and ball-skill workshops at Clifton Hill Sports Centre

- fun half-days during the summer holidays, which give children opportunities to canoe, play tennis and football with the guidance of experienced local coaches. The purpose of these taster sessions is to encourage the children regularly to access local sporting activities.

NOTE: Some group activities, consisting of adapted PE groups under the guidance of a special educational needs PE adviser are organised within mainstream schools.

Figure 8.11: Co-operative games are fun.

Other support provided by the Vranch House team

- Written exercise programmes for home and/or school

- advice about, and provision of, special equipment

- liaison with, and advice to, schools, usually via the SENCO

- liaison with the social services, in particular with the child's community occupational therapist, regarding specialist equipment at home or in school

- regular contact with parents

- co-ordination of medical and educational services – for example, organising reports from therapy and school staff for paediatric clinics, or arranging for the therapist to contribute to Statements of Special Educational Needs and annual reviews.

More about group activities

PE GROUPS

The PE skills programme includes work on ball skills, movement, balance and co-ordination.[2] The Persil Funfit scheme is used as a basis, and activities are defined under three areas: action, balance and co-ordination. The children can achieve bronze, silver and gold badges and certificates when they have achieved certain skills. The scheme was co-written by representatives from the British Amateur Gymnastics Association and the British Council of Physical Education (see Appendix 1 for details).

SWIMMING GROUPS

The Halliwick method of swimming is used (see p.81). The children work at different levels to obtain badges and certificates.

FINE MOTOR GROUPS

The fine motor groups work on hand-function skills. Activities include improving handwriting skills, craft work such as making greeting cards and collages, and cooking. When handwriting is being worked on the child's posture and pencil grip are monitored. Memory games which involve observational skills are also played, such as Kim's Game, in which the children are shown a tray holding a number of objects for a short period and then on a second presentation they have to spot which objects have been

---

2   Persil Funfit consists of a programme of activities to improve the health and general well-being of the children. The programme is non-competitive and is designed to show what children of *all* abilities can achieve.

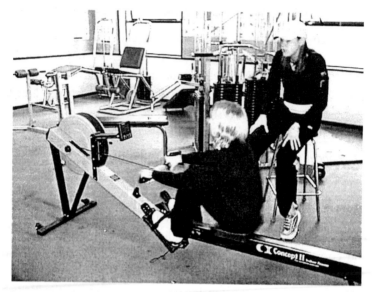

Figure 8.12: Using the multigym.

Figure 8.13: A game in the pool.

removed. Other exercises are carried out that are designed to improve visual-perceptual skills.

The benefits of therapy

Children often develop greater confidence when they find they are able to do something they could not do previously. This confidence can often transfer to other settings such as school and home.

SOPHIE, AGED 7

She has been attending for about 18 months. 'Sophie used to be very, very quiet and she's much more outgoing now – she's much more confident. That is definitely since she's been going into Vranch House, she's really come out of her shell. She'd sort of hide behind me, if anyone spoke to her, now she'll be at the door shouting out "Hello" to the neighbours.'

EMMA, AGED 10

Emma has also been attending for about 18 months. 'She's gained a lot of confidence since she's been in Vranch House. She went in first for a week's course in the August in the summer holidays, and did just the week. The first day she went in, she was awfully nervous about going in when we left her. When we came back she got in the car and said "There are bigger boys there than I am and they can't write either." She just changed once she found out there were other children who could not do things. In school they used to colour and write and used to go ahead of her, all the young ones, and she was getting left behind.'

Previously her mother reported that Emma was unwilling to attend her primary school, but now she is quite enthusiastic about going to school and her self-confidence has improved.

PAUL, AGED 8

He has been attending for two years. Paul refused to go to school during his first term. When he started at Vranch House he was six years old, and 'It used to be the highlight of his week.' He has learned to swim and is very confident in water. His primary school also now understand his difficulties, and he has had additional support from a learning support assistant. Now he is working well in school and his maths and reading have both improved.

LISA, AGED 9

Lisa has been attending for over three years. Her mother reports that her PE skills have improved and also her swimming ability. 'I mean, she's been swimming at Vranch for so long and that's one area where she really outshines Caroline [her younger sister], and it's just so lovely for her to have that one thing she is really good at and that Caroline finds more difficult.' She also said that Lisa's self-esteem has improved and that this has become more apparent as she has become older, even though the demands of school have become greater.

NOTE: The children in the photographs all attend Vranch House Centre. They all have movement difficulties which may be due to dyspraxia or other conditions.

CHAPTER 9

Leaving School

Does the dyspraxia continue as a young person matures? Portwood (1998) says 'Dyspraxia is not a condition that one simply "grows out of". Dyspraxic children become dyspraxic adults. Intervention can be effective at any age' (p.17). Researchers have come up with differing results in long-term studies.

Losse *et al.* (1991) carried out a study of 17 children identified by teachers as having poor motor co-ordination at six years of age and followed up again at 16. 'The results suggest that the majority of children still have difficulties with motor co-ordination, have poor self-concept and are experiencing problems of various kinds in school' (p.67). However, they reported differences in the ways that individual children learned coping strategies to deal with their difficulties.

Cantell, Smyth and Ahonen (1994) carried out a similar study in Finland, identifying children at 5 years of age and following up 81 of them at 15. They found that over half did not differ significantly from the control group: they were performing well in school, were ambitious and were taking part in social sports. Although they were still found to have some difficulties with motor tasks, some of the young people in this group were very keen on team sports and had spent a great deal of time taking part in them. The other 46 per cent differed from the control group on both motor and perceptual tasks. This group had fewer social activities, lower academic ambitions and poorer self-esteem.

So it is likely that many dyspraxic children do overcome their early motor difficulties and develop coping strategies to deal effectively with organisational problems, but some do not. None of the children in the Losse *et al.* study took part in long-term intervention programmes, and it is not clear whether the Finnish children did so. Nowadays there is far greater awareness of dyspraxia and movement difficulties, so it is to be hoped that many more children will succeed, become more confident and develop good self-esteem. One of the most often expressed comments from Vranch House parents is that, following an intervention pro-gramme, their child has become more self-confident both at home and at school.

Leaving school and beyond

The young dyspraxic adult is likely to avoid doing any jobs, hobbies or other activities that involve things that are difficult, such as writing, performing co-ordination skills and competitive sport. This is not unusual – most adults tend to make use of their strengths and avoid those activities that they know they do less well. The young dyspraxic person should be encouraged to develop strategies that minimise his difficulties. Sound career advice should be taken. Realistic expectations are important.

Some tips for school-leavers

Writing

Use a computer or laptop. Check out various keyboards and mice. There are many available, and you can usually try them out at local computer stores. You can get keyboards that are larger or smaller than a normal keyboard as well as specially ergonomically designed ones. Use a spellcheck programme. If you do not have speech problems try out voice-activated word-processing software.

Use a personal organiser/planner/calendar

Make a note of all appointments, personal as well as business. Use colour-coding for different appointments, e.g. dental and medical appointments in red, social arrangements in blue, work appointments in green, and so on. It's useful to keep two types of planners or organisers – a small one that you keep with you at all times, and a larger one for your kitchen or bedroom wall. Use highlighters or stickers for the colours.

Allow plenty of time

Make sure you set your alarm to give you plenty of time to get ready in the mornings. Plan your routes to work or business appointments to make sure you have enough time. Get your clothes and the things you need to take for work or college ready the night before.

Use notepads or a tape-recorder

- Keep a notepad by your bed in case things you have forgotten come to you in the middle of the night.

- Make shopping lists. Go round the kitchen and check what you need before you go shopping.

- If you are going on holiday write down everything you need to take with you.

- If you find it tiring to write or your writing is difficult to read, use a small tape-recorder.

Exercise regularly and keep fit

You may never play competitive football or cricket, but there are many other ways of keeping fit which are non-competitive but enjoyable:

- walking – especially with a dog
- rambling – join a ramblers' club
- swimming
- doing a personal fitness programme at your local gym
- cycling

- jogging
- yoga and relaxation exercises.

Be positive!

Concentrate on the things you do well. Everyone has different strengths and weaknesses. We cannot all walk tightropes or swing from trapezes, but we can all make the best of our talents. We can also contribute to society in a positive way. Do some voluntary work for a charity or help out at the local day centre for the elderly. People who have struggled to overcome difficulties themselves often have a special understanding of those who are disadvantaged in some way.

Useful Information

Government publications

Department for Education (1994) *Special Educational Needs – a Guide for Parents.*

This booklet explains the procedure of statutory assessment, Statements of Special Educational Needs, annual reviews and Special Educational Needs Tribunals. There is a very helpful list of addresses and telephone numbers at the back of the leaflet, including those of advisory and help centres and special interest groups. Available from: DfEE Publications, PO Box 5050, Sudbury, Suffolk CO10 6ZQ. Tel. 0845 602 2260.

Department of Education and Employment (1998) *Meeting Special Educational Needs. A Programme of Action.*

This document sets out the government's plans for special educational needs up to 2001, including the introduction of a simplified SEN Code of Practice. Available in full and summary versions. Ref.: *MSENPAS*, from the above address, or on the Internet at http://www.open.gov.uk/dfee/sen/senhome.htm

Department for Education and Employment (1999) *How Is Your Child Doing at School?*

A short leaflet explaining Key Stage 1, 2 and 3 assessment in 2000 and 2001. Usually updated annually. Ref.: NB ISBN 1 84185 181 7. Available from: DfEE Publications, PO Box 5050, Annesley, Nottingham NG15 0DJ. Tel. 0845 602 2260.

Qualifications and Curriculum Authority (1998) *Is Your Child about to Start School?*

A short leaflet explaining Baseline Assessment. Ref.: QCA/98/131. Available from: Qualifications and Curriculum Authority, Newcombe House, 45 Notting Hill Gate, London W11 3JB. Tel. 020 8867 333. http://www.open.gov.uk/qca/

Home therapy programme

Pinderfields and Pontefract Hospitals NHS Trust (1999) *Pindora's Box.*

A scheme developed by the paediatric occupational therapy and physiotherapy services at Pinderfields Hospital, designed to help in the training of the fine and gross motor skills of children aged 5–10. To be used under the guidance of the child's physiotherapist as a home programme. Available from Jenx Ltd, Nutwood 28, Limestone Cottage Lane, Sheffield S6 1NJ. Tel 0114 2853376.

Special equipment

Various equipment

Dycem mats in various sizes and shapes, also available in rolls (lengths can be cut off); pencil grips; triangular pencils; Plastazote tubing (supplied in 1-metre lengths, and can be cut to size and used to provide a larger grip for pencils, pens, brushes, cutlery; various scissors, including spring-loaded and dual-control. All available from: Nottingham Rehab Supplies, Ludlow Hill Road, West Bridgford, Nottingham NG2 6HD. General enquiries 0115 936 0322. Customer services 0115 936 0324/0239/0527/0238.

WriteAngle sloping table-top boards: clear perspex, portable, fixed-height writing slope. Available from: Posturite (UK) Ltd, PO Box 468, Hailsham, East Sussex BN27 4LZ. Tel. 01323 847777.

Computer roller-balls

Microspeed KIDTRAC. Three colour-coded buttons.
Microspeed PCTRAC. Grey 'age-neutral', but has three buttons like the KIDTRAC.

These two roller-balls have a 'drag-lock' feature: pressing the drag button locks it and the button stays locked until it is pressed again. Both available from: Inclusive Technology, Saddleworth Business Centre, Delph, Oldham OL3 5DF. Tel. 01457 819790.

Kids' Ball.

A large trackball with large left and right selection buttons. Available from: Granada Learning Ltd, Granada Television, Quay Street, Manchester M60 9EA. Tel. 0161 827 2927.

Fellowes Roller-ball.

A simple roller-ball with left and right selection buttons. Available from: RM Learning Systems, New Mill House, 183 Milton Park, Abingdon, Oxon OX14 4SE. Tel. 01235 826000.

DynaMyte Augmentative Communication Device.

DynaMyte is a lightweight, easy-to-carry augmentative communication device to help people with speech and communication difficulties to talk to others. Details from: Dynamic Abilities Ltd, The Coach House, 134 Purewell, Christchurch, Dorset BH23 1EU. Tel. 01202 481818.

Ideas for PE

Persil Funfit National Curriculum Resource Pack

For physical education for Key Stages 1 and 2. Also Funfit 0 to 5. The Key Stages 1 and 2 Funfit pack is due to be replaced by an updated scheme after December 2000. Information available on all Funfit schemes from: BAGA Despatch Department, Ghyll Print Ltd, Ghyll Industrial Estate, Heathfield, East Sussex TN21 8AW. Tel. 01435 866210.

E. Knight. (1992) *Special Needs Activities.*

Curriculum Services for Physical Education, Hertfordshire County Council. A booklet of flipcards giving ideas for PE in school. Available from: Action Point, Wheathampstead Education Centre, Butterfield Road, Wheathampstead, Herts AL4 8PY. Tel. 01582 830251.

Books for action-and-movement songs

B. Harrop, L. Friend and D. Gadsby (1976) *Okki-tocki-unga.* London: A. & C. Black.

Action songs for children with piano accompaniment.

B. Harrop, P. Blakely and D. Gadsby (1975) *Apuskidu.* London: A. & C. Black.

Songs for children with piano accompaniment. Not specifically action or movement songs, but some can be used in this way, e.g. 'If you're happy and you know it', 'Ten in the bed', 'One potato, two potato'.

E. Matterson (1991) *This Little Puffin.* London: Penguin Books.

Contains a large number of action-and-movement songs and rhymes; the songs have simple melody lines written out, not full accompaniment.

Useful Addresses

The Advisory Centre for Education

ACE is an independent national education advice centre which offers confidential advice to parents. It also publishes a number of guides and handbooks relating to various areas of education, including *Tribunal Toolkit* (advice on going to the Special Educational Needs Tribunal) and *The Special Education Handbook*, which explains the Code of Practice. Advisory Centre for Education, 1b Aberdeen Studios, 22–24 Highbury Grove, London N5 2DQ. ACE advice service 020 7354 8321 (Monday to Friday, 2–5pm).

AFASIC

AFASIC represents children and young adults with communication impairments. The organisation provides support for parents, carers and professionals working with these children through conferences, activity weeks, summer schools, regular newsletters and local support groups. AFASIC, 69–85 Old Street, London EC1V 9HX. Tel. 020 7841 8900. Helpline. 0845 3555577 (for parents, local call rate).

The Centre for Studies on Inclusive Education

The CSIE gives information and advice about inclusive education. Its activities include working directly with parents, producing publications and free literature about inclusion, organising conferences and answering queries on the law. Centre for Studies on Inclusive Education, 1 Redland Close, Elm Lane, Redland, Bristol BS6 6UE. Tel. 0117 923 8450.

The Children's Legal Centre

This organisation gives free advice and information about the laws and policies that affect children. The Children's Legal Centre, University of Essex, Wivenhoe Park, Colchester, Essex CO4 3SQ. Advice line 01206 873820/872466 (Monday to Friday, 2–5pm, and Monday, Wednesday and Friday, 10am–12 noon).

Contact a Family

Contact a Family aims to encourage mutual support between families whose children have disabilities and special needs by linking them through support groups and newsletters. Contact a Family, 170 Tottenham Court Road, London WIP 0HA. Tel. 020 7383 3555.

The Dyscovery Centre

The centre offers assessment, treatment and teaching for children, adolescents and adults with dyspraxia and dyslexia. The Dyscovery Centre, 12 Cathedral Road, Cardiff CF1 9LJ. Tel. 029 2022 2011.

The Dyspraxia Foundation

The Dyspraxia Foundation aims to promote the awareness and understanding of dyspraxia and to support individuals and families affected by it. The organisation has local groups across the United Kingdom and publishes a regular newsletter. The Dyspraxia Foundation, 8 West Alley, Hitchin, Herts SG5 1EG. Tel. 01462 455016 (administration). Helpline 01462 454986 (Monday to Friday, 10am–12 noon).

The Halliwick Association of Swimming Therapy

This organisation arranges courses to train instructors in the methodology and knows where Halliwick swimming is taught in an area. The Halliwick Association of Swimming Therapy, c/o The ADKC Centre, Whitstable House, Silchester Road, London W10 6SB. Tel. 020 8968 7609.

The Independent Panel for Special Education Advice

IPSEA gives independent advice on LEAs' legal duties towards children with special educational needs, free professional opinions for parents who disagree with an LEA's assessment of their child's special educational needs, and free representation at the Special Educational Needs Tribunal. IPSEA, 22 Warren Hill Road, Woodbridge, Suffolk IP12 4DU. Advice line 01394 382814 (Monday to Thursday, 10am–4pm, and Tuesday, Wednesday and Thursday, 7–9pm).

The National Association of Special Educational Needs

The aims of NASEN are to promote the interests of those with exceptional learning needs and/or disabilities; to provide a forum for those actively involved with exceptional learning needs and/or disabilities; and to contribute to the formulation and development of policy. NASEN publishes two journals and a magazine/newsletter. NASEN House, 4–5 Amber Business Village, Amber Close, Amington, Tamworth B77 4RP. Tel. 01827 311500.

The National Portage Association

Portage is a home-visiting service for pre-school children with special needs. Portage home visitors assess children's needs and work together with parents on a home-based teaching programme. The National Portage Association, 127 Monks Dale, Yeovil, Somerset BA21 3JE. Tel. 01935 471641.

Network 81

Network 81 is a national organisation of parents of children with special educational needs and gives advice on various issues relating to education such as statementing and the Code of Practice. Network 81, 1–7 Woodfield Terrace, Chapel Hill, Stansted, Essex CM24 8AJ. Helpline 01279 647415 (Monday to Friday, 10am–2pm).

The PAL Centre (Dyslexia and Dyspraxia Parent-assisted Learning)

This organisation offers assessments and home programmes for dyslexic and dyspraxic children. The PAL Centre, BIBIC (British Institute for Brain Injured Children), Knowle Hall, Bridgwater, Somerset TA7 8PJ. Tel. 01278 684060.

Parents for Inclusion

Parents for Inclusion is an association of parents of children with disabilities who believe in all children's entitlement to a good education in their local mainstream school. The helpline is run by trained parents to advise other parents on issues relating to inclusion. Parents for Inclusion, Unit 2, Ground Floor, 70 South Lambeth Road, London SW8 1RL. Tel. 020 7735 7735. Helpline 020 7582 5008 (for parents, Monday, Wednesday and Thursday, 10am–2pm).

Bibliography

American Psychiatric Association (1987) *Diagnostic and Statistical Manual of Mental Disorders* (3rd edn, rev.). Washington DC: American Psychiatric Association.

Ayres, A.J. (1972) *Sensory Integration and Learning Disorders.* Los Angeles: Western Psychological Services.

Barnett, R., Hall, J.D., Kirkby, G.B., Makin, R., Price, D.M. and Williams, D.H. (1989) *Physical Education for Children with Special Educational Needs in Mainstream Education.* Leeds: British Association of Advisers and Lecturers in Physical Education.

Beery, K.E. (1989) *The VMI. Developmental Test of Visual-Motor Integration.* Cleveland, ON: Modern Curriculum Press.

Boon, M. (1993) *The Integration of Statemented Special Needs Pupils in Ordinary Schools in Lancashire.* MSc thesis, University of Lancaster.

Cantell, M.H., Smyth, M., and Ahonen, T.P. (1994) 'Clumsiness in adolescence: educational, motor, and social outcomes of motor delay detected at 5 years.' *Adapted Physical Activity Quarterly 11*, 2, 115–129.

Clark, C.R., Davies, C.O., and Woodcock, R.W. (1974) *Standard Rebus Glossary.* Minneapolis, MN: American Guidance Service.

Connery, V.M., *et al.* (1985, 1992) *The Nuffield Centre Dyspraxia Programme.* London: The Nuffield Hearing and Speech Centre.

Department for Education (1994a) *Code of Practice on the Identification and Assessment of Special Educational Needs.* London: Central Office of Information.

Department for Education (1994b) *Special Educational Needs – a Guide for Parents.* London: Central Office of Information.

Dixon, N.F. (1972) 'The beginings of preception.' In B.M. Foss (ed) *New Horizons in Psychology 1.* Harmondsworth: Penguin Books.

Dorland, W.A.N. (1947) *The American Illustrated Medical Dictionary* (21st edn). Philadelphia, PA: W. B. Saunders Co.

Dussart, G. (1994) Identifying the clumsy child in school: an exploratory study. *British Journal of Special Education 21*, 2, 81–86.

Dyspraxia Foundation (1998) *Developmental Dyspraxia Explained.* Hitchin: Dyspraxia Foundation.

Gardner, M.F. (1982) *TVPS. Test of Visual-Perceptual Skills (Non-motor).* San Francisco, CA: Psychological and Educational Publications, Inc.

Gibson, E.J. and Walk, R.D. (1960) 'The visual cliff.' *Scientific American 202*, 4, 64–71.

Goodenough, F.L. (1926) *Measurement of Intelligence by Drawings.* Chicago: Harcourt, Brace & World Inc.

Gordon, N. and McKinlay, I. (1980) *Helping Clumsy Children.* Edinburgh: Churchill Livingstone.

Grove, N. and Walker, M. (1990) *The Makaton Vocabulary. Using Manual Signs and Graphic Symbols to Develop Interpersonal Communication. AAC: Augmentative and Alternative Communication.* Baltimore, MD: Williams & Wilkins.

Harriman, P.L. (1947) *The New Dictionary of Psychology.* New York: Philosophical Library Inc.

Harris, D.B. (1963) *Children's Drawings as Measures of Intellectual Maturity (A Revision and Extension of the Goodenough Draw-a-man Test).* New York, Chicago and Burlingame: Harcourt, Brace & World Inc.

Hehner, B. (1980) *Blissymbols for Use.* Toronto, ON: Blissymbolics Communication Institute.

Henderson, S.E., and Sugden, D. A. (1992) *The Movement Assessment Battery for Children.* Sidcup: Psychological Corporation, Harcourt Brace Jovanovich.

Kirby, A. (1999) *Dyspraxia. The Hidden Handicap.* London: Souvenir Press.

Knight, E. (1992) *Special Needs Activities.* Wheathampstead: Curriculum Services for Physical Education, Hertfordshire County Council.

Losse, A., Henderson, S.E., Elliman, D., Hall, D., Knight, E., and Jongmans, M. (1991) 'Clumsiness in children – do they grow out of it? A 10-year follow-up study.' *Developmental Medicine and Child Neurology 33*, 55–68.

Macintyre, C. (2000) *Dyspraxia in the Early Years.* London: David Fulton Publishers.

Mayer-Johnson, R. (1989) *The Picture Communication Symbols I and II combined.* Solana Beach, CA: Mayer-Johnson Co.

McKinlay, I. (1998) 'Foreword: What Is "Dyspraxia"?' In R. Hunt (ed), *Praxis Makes Perfect II.* Hitchin: Dyspraxia Foundation.

Nash-Wortham, M. and Hunt, J.C. (1997) *Take Time.* Stourbridge: Robinswood Press.

O'Beirne, C., Larkin, D. and Cable, T. (1994) 'Co-ordination problems and anaerobic performance in children.' *Adapted Physical Activity Quarterly 11*, 2, 141–149.

Pinderfields and Pontefract Hospitals NHS Trust (1999) *Pindora's Box.* Sheffield: Jenx Ltd.

Portwood, M. (1996) *Developmental Dyspraxia. A Manual for Parents and Professionals.* Durham: Durham County Council.

Portwood, M. (1998) 'Developmental dyspraxia – identification, assessment and intervention.' In R. Hunt (ed), *Praxis Makes Perfect II*. Hitchin: Dyspraxia Foundation.

Portwood, M. (1999) *Developmental Dyspraxia. Identification and Intervention. A Manual for Parents and Professionals.* London: David Fulton Publishers.

Ripley, K., Daines, B., and Barrett, J. (1997) *Dyspraxia. A Guide for Teachers and Parents.* London: David Fulton Publishers.

Rosenthal, J. and McCabe, T. (1999) *Dyspraxia Information Sheet. Disorders* 8, 16–26. University of Sydney, Australia.
http://www.cchs-usyd-edu.au/Academic/CD/Clinic/dyspraxia.html

Roussounis, S.H., Gaussen, T.H. and Stratton, P. (1987) 'A 2-year follow-up study of children with motor co-ordination problems identified at school entry age.' *Child: Care, Health and Development 13*, 377–391.

Sassoon, R. (1998) 'Dealing with Handwriting Problems.' In R. Hunt (ed), *Praxis Makes Perfect II*. Hitchin: Dyspraxia Foundation.

Shapiro, B. (1991) 'To Understand Dyspraxia.' In R. Hunt (ed), *Praxis Makes Perfect II*. Hitchin: Dyspraxia Foundation.

Stott, D.H., Moyes, F.A., and Henderson, S.E. (1984) *Test of Motor Impairment: Henderson Revision.* San Antonia, TX: Psychological Corporation.

Sylvester, S. (1999) *Dyspraxia Evaluation 1999.* Barnstaple: North Devon Health Trust.

Walker, M. (1976) *The Makaton Vocabulary.* Camberley: Makaton Vocabulary Project.

Wechsler, D. (1990) *Wechsler Pre-school and Primary Scale of Intelligence – Revised UK Edition (WPPSI-RUK).* London: Psychological Corporation.

Wechsler, D. (1992) *Wechsler Intelligence Scale for Children – Third UK Edition (WISC-IIIUK).* London: Psychological Corporation.

Wedell, K. (1973) *Learning and Perceptuo-motor Disabilities in Children.* London: John Wiley & Sons.

Williams, C.A., Smith, J. and Ainsley, J. (1999) 'The effects of a physiotherapy intervention programme on children with developmental co-ordination disorder.' *Association of Paediatric Chartered Physiotherapists Journal 91*, 32–40.

Subject Index

Author Index